DOVE

Robin Lee Graham
with Derek L.T. Gill

HARPER  PERENNIAL

NEW YORK • LONDON • TORONTO • SYDNEY

Dove

Author's Note

I would like to thank Derek Gill for all the hours he spent in helping me write *Dove*. Without his help this book would never have been written.

I would also like to thank my father, Lyle Graham, for having enough faith in me to make this trip possible and my mother, Norma Graham, for having the courage to stand by his decision.

My sincere thanks go to the many people who prayed for me along this trip, for I now know that it was their faith in God that saw me through safely.

And last but not least my loving thanks to my wife, Patricia, for all of her encouragement.

HARPER ● PERENNIAL

This back was originally published in hardcover in 1972 by Harper & Row, Publishers, Inc.

First HarperPerennial edition published 1991.

LIBRARY OF CONGRESS CATALOG CARD NUMBER 78-181623

ISBN 0-06-092047-5

09 RRD(H)   50 49 48 47 46 45 44

Contents

Illustrations follow pages 52 and 120.

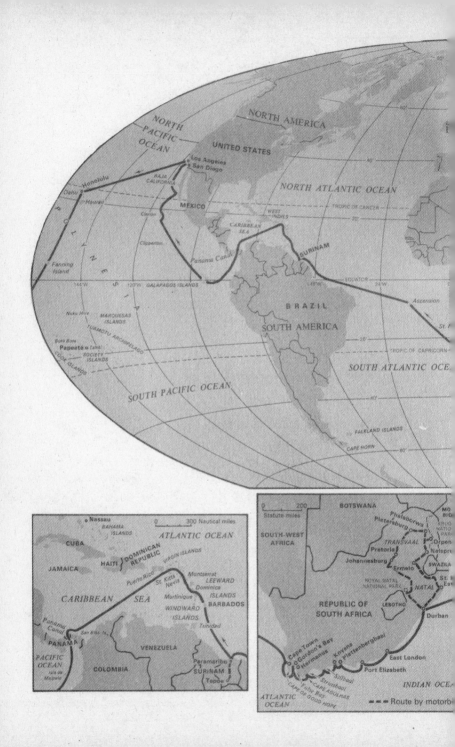

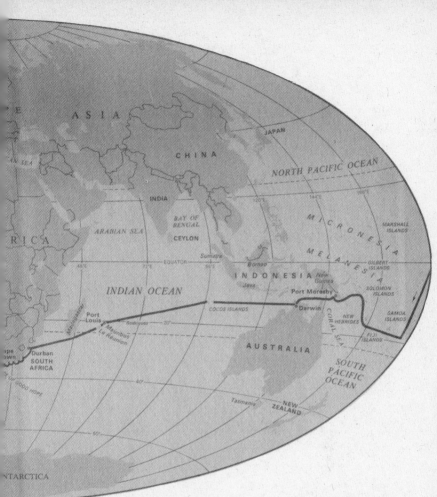

The Voyage of the Dove

～～ 1

Joining the Circle

DOVE nosed into her slip at the Long Beach marina, her sails furled like a bird resting its wings after a storm. I wasn't thinking about the voyage at all. My mind was on Patti. I was yearning to hold her again. She was standing there among the reporters and television cameras, and laughing—her long wheat-colored hair blowing across her face in that familiar way, her body swollen with my child.

As Dove was being tied up, so many newsmen came charging down the floating slip that it threatened to sink and to throw them into the April-chill water. I sat on the cabin roof waiting for the customs officer, and a dozen microphones were thrust into my face. Then the questions came at me like stones.

"What does it feel like to be the youngest sailor to have circled the world single-handed?"

"I haven't given it much thought," I said—and that was true.

"Would you do it again?"

"God no! I've done it once. Why do it again?"

"How did Patti become pregnant?" This from a woman reporter fluttering artificial eyelashes.

I urged her to read a book on birds and bees. She was closer than she knew to a love story that I wasn't yet ready to tell.

"What did you think about when you were alone and a thousand miles from land?"

"Perhaps the things you think about when you're alone," I parried, "but mostly about the next port."

"How far have you traveled since leaving California five years ago?"

"About thirty thousand and six hundred miles," I said.

"What are you going to do now?"

"Take a hot bath."

"Did you do it for a stunt?"

"A stunt! Hell no!"

Patti was making signs to me, trying to tell me to keep my cool. She knew how short my fuse was when people asked damn-fool questions. But how could I tell these people, all thinking of their copy deadlines, why I had made this voyage?

Couldn't they leave me alone? Couldn't they guess that all I wanted was to be with Patti, to get away from this damned boat, to be among trees again, and in front of a blazing hearth and in a bed that didn't lurch with every wave and wind?

Actually I had seen Patti half an hour earlier. She and her father and my parents had come out in a launch at dawn to meet *Dove* at the breakwater. Patti had leaned perilously over the launch's rail to give me a breakfast of fresh melon, hot rolls and a bottle of champagne. I had drunk the whole bottle before reaching the marina and my mood was reasonably mellow. The reporters were safe. I even grinned at them. The television cameras zoomed in.

Many have sailed long and dangerous voyages for the sake of personal glory. Others have sailed for personal adventure. I fall into neither group. I have tried to answer honestly when people have asked me what made me do it—what compelled me at the age of sixteen to take a twenty-four-foot sailboat out of San Pedro harbor (it flanks Long Beach) and to tell my family and friends, "I'm going around the world."

Shakespeare, who seems to have had an answer to most questions, had Hamlet say, "There's a divinity that shapes our ends, rough-hew them how we will." That was an answer that fitted pretty closely.

I'd never heard of Shakespeare and understood nothing about destiny when I went to school at the age of five in California. The classroom was close to a forest of yacht masts, and while other kids crayoned pictures of automobiles, airplanes, flowers or their Uncle Harry wearing big glasses, I drew only pictures of boats—boats with scores of portholes, top-heavy boats, small boats, wind-filled mainsails, mizzens, genoas, jibs and spinnakers. Then, when I was ten and a lot more resentful of homework, I pressured my father into giving me an eight-foot dinghy—beat up but beautiful. We were living then at Morro Bay, one of the more attractive of California's coastal towns. On launching day my father said he would teach me how to sail. He was full of wisdom because the previous night he had been reading a manual titled *How to Handle a Small Craft*. We got out two hundred yards from the shore and he lectured me on the danger of jibing (page 16 in the manual). Hardly had he lowered his finger than the boat jibed and both of us were thrown into the water.

But how I loved that little boat. Every day when school was over my brother Michael would dash off to the back yard and tinker with his beach buggy, but I would run all the way to the little wooden jetty beyond the reeds near our house. Sailing already meant much more to me than "mucking about in boats," as the neighbors used to call it. It was the chance to escape from blackboards and the smell of disinfectant in the school toilet, from addition and subtraction sums that were never the same as the teacher's answers, from spelling words like "seize" and "fulfill" and from little league baseball. It was the chance to be alone and to be as free for a while as the sea gulls that swung around Morro Rock.

One night when I should have been asleep I could hear my parents talking about me, their voices drifting down the passage from the living room. "I'm worried that he's such a loner," said my mother. "He needs more company. More friends. Perhaps we should ask Stephen or David to join us for the vacation."

A loner? Was I really different? I had friends. But I liked being alone, and a boat gave me the chance of getting away from people.

Was I different just because history didn't turn me on and boats did? Perhaps sailing is in the genes. Ten years before I was born, my father and his brother had started to build a twenty-eight-foot boat, intending to sail it around the world. They had the hull finished and were beginning to study the charts of Polynesia when the headlines blazed Pearl Harbor. When I was thirteen my father still had ideas of fulfilling his boyhood dream; or at least part of it. He had made out well with his house construction and real estate business. One day he took me to the Long Beach marina and as we walked past a thirty-six-foot ketch with a "For Sale" sign pinned to its stern I crawled under the green canvas. When my father called me I invited him to climb aboard. I don't know whether it was at this moment that my father decided to buy the *Golden Hind*, but a few days later he told the family that he had sold his business and that we were all going sailing in the South Seas.

My father is a quiet man, wiry, not by appearance the adventurous type, and his decision seemed on the surface out of character. Anyway, at the age of thirteen I was not going to analyze his motives or his personality (although I guess my mother did). For me the prospect of missing school for a year and sailing over that horizon was not one to be questioned.

We spent three months equipping the *Golden Hind*, provisioning her with six hundred cans of food, and then, without fanfare but with much head shaking from our kin, we sailed south to Nuku Hiva, the port of entry to the Marquesas islands. Fortunately bad memories fade fast and the happiest stay in the forefront of our minds. I can barely recall, for instance, our eighteen days in the doldrums or my being doubled up with a flaring appendix about 120 miles from the nearest surgeon in Papeete. The appendectomy wound failed to heal, and I spent three weeks in a primitive hospital where huge cockroaches crawled up the wall.

But I did remember, and always will, the deep blue of the coral lagoons, the Tahitian girls wearing *pereus* in Gauguin colors. I remember the girls running down golden beaches, their arms filled with exotic flowers and fresh fruit wrapped in palm fronds.

On one of the islands, Rangiroa, a Tahitian family called on my parents and, straight-faced, offered to trade me for two of their daughters, Joliette and Suzette. The barter proposal boosted my ego, and I did my best to persuade my parents to accept the offer, figuring that surfing in the Tuamotu Archipelago and living off coconut milk and manioc roots amounted to a better life style than learning geometry and eating hamburgers.

But my parents shook their heads and we sailed the *Golden Hind* to Huahine, Tahaa, Bora Bora, the Cook Islands and Pago Pago before heading northeast to Hawaii. At fifteen I was back in a California classroom, my spelling still lousy, but I was almost as useful with a sextant as a veteran sailor. On our eleven-thousand-mile voyage I had seen lands of unbelievable enchantment.

It is hard to believe that my parents, having allowed me to sail the South Seas at a most impressionable age, could ever have expected me to be a typical American schoolkid, to go on to college and graduate to a walnut office desk, a home on Acacia Avenue and membership in the local golf club.

I am sure Corona del Mar's high school is a good one. For me it was a return to prison. Beyond its asphalt playground and wired fences there were sun-splashed, palm-fringed shores waiting for my shadow.

A chance to take to the sea came again when two school friends —Jud Croft and Pete Tupas—and I pressured a Costa Mesa yacht-builder to allow us to deliver a new boat to a buyer in Hawaii. But three days before we were due to set sail on the 2,200-mile voyage the yachtbuilder called off the arrangement. I think he was afraid of bad publicity if our voyage failed.

Aware of my bitterness, my father invited me to be his mate on a voyage to Hawaii on his new boat, *Valerie*, a thirty-foot ketch. Keeping watch turn and turn about and weathering half a dozen squalls, we made the trip in twenty-seven days. One incident of this voyage stays in my mind. A bagged genoa, poorly lashed, broke loose and slithered across the forward deck into the ocean. We turned *Valerie* about but just as we came within grappling range the bag began to sink. Under a few inches of clear water the bag looked like a human body. A portion of the sail had escaped and took the form of a face, white and quite terrifying.

I had never seen a person drown (and pray heaven I never will) but in watching the sinking canvas bag I gained a great respect for the sea. I understood for the first time that blue water is not an innocent and sparkling playground but that it can destroy mercilessly.

We arrived in Hawaii without further incident and I was packed off to McKinley High School. My mother was to join us in a month or two. This was my sixth school and I had to make new friends again. At McKinley I found two brothers, Jim and Arthur, who loved sailing as much as I did. Jim and I were fifteen and Art a year younger. Together we invested our savings of one hundred dollars in an old sixteen-foot aluminum lifeboat. During the school lunch break the three of us would meet secretively in the shade of a palm tree and talk about our boat, which we named *HIC*—for reasons we need not go into. One lunch hour, the idea was born of sailing *HIC* to the Hawaiian island of Lanai. Jim had been reading *The Adventures of Tom Sawyer* as a class assignment and I contributed stories of the South Sea island girls who wore hibiscus in their hair. The upshot was a top-secret plan to sail to some distant isolated cove. To provision *HIC* I made a few dollars by diving in Ala Wai harbor and salvaging material from a sunken yacht.

As our plans developed, school became almost unbearable. It wasn't so much that I disliked learning—for I realized the need to be at least partially civilized and my grades were average—but that I detested the routine of school days, the unchanging pattern from the brushing of my teeth to learning English grammar. I came to hate the sound of the bell that summoned me to class, the smell of tennis shoes and sweat in the gym, the drone of history lessons, the threat of tests and exams.

Down at Ala Wai harbor it was all so different. I loved the smell of rope and resin, even of diesel oil. I loved the sound of water slapping hulls, the whip of halyards against tall masts. These were the scents and sounds of liberty and life.

It was the week that Winston Churchill died that Jim, Art and I decided it was time to sail. Maybe that old warrior had something to do with our decision. The radio and newspapers poured out stories of the "Man of the Century"—the swashbuckling states-man-soldier with a bulldog jaw who had defied Fuzzy-Wuzzies, tyrants and convention. My own tyrants were peanut butter sand-wiches and people in gloomy offices who insisted I wear shoes, people determined to arrange my life in tidy patterns, prodding me this way and that until I could be safely sent out into society, wearing white collars and gray suits, credit cards in my billfold, golf clubs in the closet under the stairs and a half-paid-for car in the garage.

Yes, I think Winston Churchill can take some responsibility for what happened next.

HIC's hull was as patched as a sailor's pants, and where some rivets were missing we filled up the holes with chewing gum, which was a lot cheaper than the filling material on sale in the marine shops. To change the craft into a sailboat, we bolted on a plywood keel, stepped a salvaged boom for a mast and stayed it with bits of rigging found lying around the yacht club. The sails were old, cut-down throwaways from a ketch.

On the evening of Thursday, January 28, 1965, Jim, Art and I tore pages from our school notebooks and wrote letters to our parents. The letters, we made sure, would not be received before we were on the high seas. To my father (my mother was visiting in California) I wrote:

Dear Dad,

Sorry for leaving without saying good-bye. But if I had done so you would not have let me go. I want to thank you for raising me as you have done. I think a father could not have done a better job. Sorry, too, for taking some of your goods. I have written to Mom to ask her to send you my money in my savings bank at Newport. Don't worry about me. I'll be all right. I miss you and love you very much.

Love, Lee

(My parents usually called me Lee.)

My father had been suffering from a cold so I added: "Hope you feel better real soon."

The veteran sailor knows better than to leave on a Friday. We were not veterans and immediately after school we rendezvoused at the yacht harbor. An hour later we cheerfully turned *HIC* toward the breakwater. Occasionally we looked astern to make sure no one was following. Then Art shouted an alarm as he spotted an outboard racing toward us. But we had not been betrayed. It was a yacht harbor friend, Chuck, the only other person who knew of our plans. He had come to wish us bon voyage and to take a couple of photographs. Chuck was shrewd enough to guess that his picture of us might have commercial value. Just before he left us, Chuck pointed with his thumb toward the small craft warning just hoisted on the breakwater.

"Should we turn back?" Art asked nervously.

"Looks like a nice day to me," said Jim, "and anyway nothing usually happens when the small craft warning is up."

"How would we explain those letters to our parents?" I asked, and that was the clincher.

I turned *HIC* toward the buoy at Diamond Head. The wind on the quarter was fresh, warm, inviting, but over the horizon there appeared an ink-black cloud, sinister as the smoke from a witch's brew. We were now too far from the harbor to see the hoisting of a second red pennant, nor did we know that the radio was putting out a full gale warning for the islands.

With a sense of high adventure, we swung *HIC* into the Molokai channel. Here the placid sea was filled with whitecaps. Art now had the tiller, but his face soon looked as green as the water. He was thoughtful enough to lean over the leeward side. In ten minutes the wind lifted from fifteen to twenty-five knots and the jib ripped along its main seam. Jim tore away the strips and hoisted a second sail. For a while *HIC* bounced jauntily across the white-caps, but when the wind continued to mount I ordered Jim to furl the mainsail.

I had had much more sailing experience than my shipmates and it seemed natural for me to take command. So far it had been the wind that had worried me, but now I began to take in the height of the swells. They were getting much too big—twenty feet from trough to crest. The second jib was suddenly torn to ribbons, and bits of canvas flew downwind like a dozen kites. The tattered stay-sail was all we had, and I had to keep *HIC*'s stern to the sea by working the rudder. By holding this course I hoped, we would at least drift toward Maui, where we could take our chances with the surf.

By late afternoon the situation was serious. Wind was gusting between twenty-five and forty knots and swells were averaging thirty feet. Jim was now lying in the bottom of the boat, wrapped about in the wet third jib. He was vomiting and crying. *HIC* was sturdier than she looked and slithered down the surface of the combers. Every now and then a big comber would smack into her stern and twenty gallons of water would thud over my back and pour across the bottom boards.

Lashing the tiller, I helped Art bale with plastic buckets. We knew well enough that another big comber would put the boat dangerously low in the water. Although *HIC* had been built as a lifeboat, the flotation tanks had long since been removed, and our funds had not allowed us to buy a raft.

There was nothing exciting about the situation now. The sense of adventure that we had carried across the harbor mouth had quite gone. Wind-whipped gray clouds scudded a few feet above our heads and our homemade rigging cracked like pistol shots as it lashed the mast. Darkness fell quickly and with our loss of vision our sense of hearing increased. The sea began to sound like a fleet of locomotives and the cold pierced our flesh like a thousand needles. I kept thinking of the plywood keel. If it broke away we would have no hope, for *HIC* would roll right over with the first broadside.

It was neither courage nor, I think, stupidity that prevented me from thinking about drowning. It was simply that all my energy and thoughts were concentrated on keeping *HIC* afloat. Art, seasick though he was, volunteered to take the tiller, but at the moment of handing it over to him a huge comber thumped our stern with a jar that threw the three of us to the floor. We jumped up spluttering and baled with all our strength.

The wind, I guessed, was now fifty knots. It was Art's idea to rig the mainsail across the boat as a spray guard. He tied one end to the mast while I lashed its edges to the gunwales. So we huddled in the darkness beneath our awning until another big comber hit and crushed the canvas to the bottom. We baled until our bodies ached with pain.

Perhaps it was the bitter cold and weariness that dulled my mind, for strangely fear never overwhelmed me. From the tiller I could see the moonlike faces of my friends as we waited for the final wave that would send us to the bottom. Sometime between midnight and dawn we heard a plane, one of several out searching for us. But by the time we had found and fired a flare, the aircraft was far away.

An hour after dawn the wind dropped sufficiently for us to hoist the spare mainsail, and our spirits rose. It was enough just to know that we had somehow survived the night. Art remembered his small transistor radio and switched it on. For a while we listened to some music and then the announcer came through with news. The first story was about us. The announcer said:

"The Coast Guard is conducting an extensive air and sea search for three teen-age boys feared to be lost at sea. The Coast Guard spokesman reports that because of the extreme weather conditions last night the chances of their survival in a sixteen-foot boat are very slim."

The report went on to give details of our families and school, and promised to report any further developments.

We listened in stunned silence, unable at first to realize that we were on the news. Then perhaps to our credit we were worried about the anxiety our families would be feeling. I wondered if my mother in California had picked up the news. It hurt me to think what she was going through. We did not then know that our adventure was the main story in the Hawaiian newspapers. It had even swept the Churchill headlines from the top of page one.

Our situation was now much better. We had food and water for several days. Then Art pointed over the side with an exclamation. Our keel had finally broken away and was drifting past the stern.

Had the keel snapped off the previous night in the height of the storm, we certainly would not have been still afloat this warm morning. But by now we knew we had made it.

By midmorning *HIC* drifted on the lee shore of Lanai. With a reefed jib we managed to steer around narrow coral heads, and before the sun had dropped the bow crunched into a sandy beach. We threw out our only anchor and staggered up the sand.

Hearing a picnic party along the shore, we stumbled over rocks and thorns to reach the circle of their firelight. The party guessed who we were at once because hourly radio bulletins had been giving ever gloomier reports about the missing teen-agers. One member of the picnic party volunteered to drive us to Lanai City, about eight miles inland. He properly urged us to report to the police.

At the police station the reception was mixed; the officer on duty was obviously pleased to see us and pushed mugs of hot coffee into our hands while telling us we were crazy. He called up the Coast Guard and reported our safety. We spent that night in jail. No drunk had ever slept better in my bunk.

Next morning a plane chartered by Jim and Art's parents flew us back to Honolulu, and it was at the airport that I first experienced a full bombardment of news reporters' questions and learned what it feels like to look down the barrels of television cameras.

My father was there too. He had his own opinion of our adventure. But he did remind me of the seafarers' superstition never to start a voyage on a Friday.

For several weeks the story of *HIC* was followed by a flood of correspondence in Hawaiian newspapers—letters signed by "Angry Taxpayer" and retired colonels who huffed and puffed about our irresponsibility. But there was one letter in the *Star-Bulletin* which I stuck into my scrapbook. It reads in part:

I am not unmindful of the staggering amount of time, effort and cost to us taxpayers which was involved in this escapade by three teenagers who sailed to Lanai in an old lifeboat. It was a pretty big goof up on their part, and I doubt very much if they are front page heroes to their friends. I am sure they now feel pretty stupid about the whole affair. But what really gets me is this trying to equate the attitude of "We wanted to see if we could do it" with your correspondents' propositions about "this dry rot affecting the youth of our nation."

Think what the elimination of the attitude of these boys would have meant to the world. Would Columbus have discovered America? Would the Wright brothers have flown at Kitty Hawk? Would Mount Everest have been climbed? Indeed would our Hawaiian ancestors have discovered these lovely islands?

A little red-blooded urge to excel, to do the impossible, to see what is over the next hill and to take little heed of the consequences—these are as American as apple-pie. It is obvious that the angry critics of these boys never walked a neighbor's fence or swam a forbidden hole or pushed over an outhouse on Hallowe'en. . . . Irresponsible? Yes. Thoughtless? Yes. But dry rot in the nation's youth? Baloney.

The letter was signed: Gene Weston.

Another correspondent, who lashed us for our "foolish escapade," expressed his gratitude that "there are a few youngsters in the country who aren't out raping, mugging and murdering . . . and whose initiative, though misguided, will help them to avoid becoming teen-age vegetables." The writer concluded, "They're a trio of crazy kids who are lucky to be alive, and they've learned this too. But don't be too quick to criticize that quality we need most in this day and age: raw guts."

Perhaps it was this more tolerant view of our adventure, which had cost $25,000 in rescue operations, that helped us when we were ordered to appear before a hearing of the local Coast Guard. We were found guilty under a federal law which prohibits the reckless or negligent operation of a vessel endangering the life, limb or property of any person, and we were assessed a one-hundred-dollar penalty each. But we were excused from payment.

The penalty was remitted by Captain Herbert J. Kelly, acting chief of the Merchant Marine Safety Division of the 14th Coast Guard, because, he stressed, the parents would have to pay for their sons' violations. Had we been convicted in a federal court we could have been sentenced to one year in a reformatory or a two-thousand-dollar fine or both. Captain Kelly gave us the ghost of a grin as he dismissed us from the courtroom.

So instead of a life on the islands—and it had been our eventual plan to sail HIC to the South Seas—we returned to McKinley High School, I to complete my sophomore year.

My father knew well enough that although my first attempt to escape from established society had failed, I intended to try again. I could not yet articulate what motivated me, but my father wrote my mother from Hawaii: "Lee is more interested in living than longevity."

I knew what I disliked, what I wanted to leave behind. But I knew too that there was something "out there" that I desperately wanted. It was a chance to be my own man, a conviction that I was born free, that I had a birthright that would not be denied.

Recognizing that I would do "some other damn silly thing in a tub like HIC," my father argued that it would be better to find me a boat that was reasonably safe for ocean sailing. Mother never accepted this reasoning, but father flew back to California and bought a twenty-four-foot fiberglass Lapworth sloop in a San Pedro boatyard. She was called Dove and carried a thirty-foot aluminum mast, a fifteen-foot boom and she drew four feet. Although five years old, Dove was in good shape, with hatches and portholes strong enough to withstand a heavy pounding.

On the first day of the summer school vacation I flew from Hawaii to join my father in California. I was now sixteen years old, and for the first time seriously considered sailing around the world. This idea was just a passing notion, but it began to nag at the back of my mind. Instead of turning my school atlas to the Polynesian islands, I flicked the pages to the maps of Australia and the Indian Ocean. The Suez Canal had not at that time been closed by the Six Day War between Israel and Egypt and I began to picture myself racing Arab dhows up the Red Sea. If I could get that far, I argued, it would be natural to sail the Mediterranean, "take in Europe" and return to Long Beach by way of the North Atlantic and the Panama Canal.

On my small atlas it all looked so straightforward, and I thought that two years would probably be time enough for the journey. I didn't worry about the cost, because with a schoolboy's optimism I expected that problem to work out somehow.

Surprisingly, my father barely reacted when I put the idea to him. We were now working ten hours a day preparing *Dove* for the ocean. I did not realize at the time that secretly my father had been hoping I would come up with just such a scheme, and that right from the beginning he would live my voyage and my life vicariously.

My father and I spent most of July companionably together fitting out *Dove*, installing a thirty-gallon fresh-water tank, constructing a stern pulpit rail, putting up heavy rigging. Then we fitted a chronometer, barometer, gimbal tray for a kerosene stove, furling gear and roller reefing for the mainsail. This furling equipment would allow me to raise and lower sails from the cockpit in seconds if I was hit by a sudden squall. Other special fittings and extras included a lifeline attached to the boom and harness, a small blow-up raft containing a compass, water and hard rations, a chart table and lockers, a David White navy sextant, a marine radio receiver and volumes one through four of the Hydrographic Office's Longitude and Latitude Tables. We put two compasses aboard, mounting one on *Dove*'s self-baling cockpit and the other, a "telltale," above the port bunk.

The most important and complex extra equipment was a wind

vane of our original design. Its operation was quite simple—the vane of about one square yard of canvas moving through a gear system, a small trim rudder which would keep Dove on course while I slept. In effect it was an automatic pilot, and although the vane would not work too well when the wind was on the beam, my charts showed that I would be traveling downwind or windward most of the time on an east-to-west global voyage.

From friends and local churches I collected about five hundred articles of used clothing. The idea was to trade these—and one hundred ballpoint pens—for food and other necessities when I reached the islands.

We invested heavily in canned food and I found room (reluctantly) for schoolbooks and a small steel bow and quiver of arrows (not to fight cannibals but to attempt to shoot fish).

Dove had originally cost $5,500, but by the time we had fitted her out with the additional equipment and provisioned her, the total investment was about $8,000—a sum, I assured my father, that was to be regarded as a loan.

In the evenings, although bone weary, I studied prevailing currents and winds and seasonal weather patterns which would determine my course.

It never occurred to me to publicize my voyage and I asked my father to keep our plans secret. But somehow word got out, perhaps through a marine shop or a friend, that a sixteen-year-old schoolboy was planning to sail the world single-handed. One morning while working on Dove I heard an unfamiliar voice on the slip. It was a reporter from a local newspaper, the San Pedro Pilot. I looked up and found him standing there, pencil poised and notebook in hand, a photographer at his shoulder. With my mind occupied with adjusting the wind vane, I thought his questions innocent enough, but the reporter, Mr. Lyle Le Faver, was the front scout of an army of newsmen who were to besiege me from that moment on.

I have nothing against newsmen. Many of them are really nice, but it seemed silly to me that even before I sailed past Catalina island, twenty miles out of Long Beach, I should be worth more than a paragraph on an inside page. Yet the report that a schoolboy was contemplating a globe-circling voyage seemed to fascinate the press, and radio and the television studios.

When I was ready to sail on the morning of July 27, I had been given almost as much publicity as a presidential candidate or a notorious gangster. I was honestly and deeply embarrassed when on sailing day the reporters and television men who turned up at the San Pedro marina outnumbered my friends and relatives almost ten to one.

Among the farewell gifts were a couple of kittens brought in a basket by my uncle, Dick Fisher, with whom my father and I had been staying. I named them immediately Joliette and Suzette for the two Tahitian girls who had been offered to my parents as a trade for me three years earlier. The kittens, born in a closet, became famous overnight, their pictures appearing on front pages from Mexico to London.

The morning of July 27, 1965, was a marvelous one, with the sun burning off the mist in the outer harbor. Excitement killed my appetite, but I sat down with Jud Croft and ate a bowl of breakfast cereal. Jill Gibson, a girl friend who had come up from Newport, delighted the cameramen by giving me a kiss.

Then my father came aboard. He looked ill at ease, uptight, and when he put out his hand I noticed it was trembling. He said something about seeing me in Hawaii. Then, at exactly ten o'clock, I started up Dove's inboard engine.

That was the beginning of it all.

I wonder now if I had been able to see the future whether I would have sailed at all. Supposing at that moment I had been able to sense the loneliness that drove me to within a breath of madness, supposing I had seen my demastings or that huge storm in the Indian Ocean—would I have left the slipway at San Pedro? Yet if I had been able to see the terrors and troubles of my global voyage I would have seen, too, the days of tremendous joy, days no man deserves this side of heaven. I would have seen Patti out there in the islands, Patti laughing, the sun on her shoulders, Patti in my arms through velvet nights. Yes, I am sure I would have sailed—sailed through hurricanes, the deepest hurts and hell itself had I known the full pattern of my life.

As it was, on that sparkling morning at San Pedro marina, setting out on the 2,225-mile first leg of my voyage around the world, my heart thumped with an excitement I had never known before —for the spirit of freedom seemed to be touching me with her wings.

2

Loneliness and Landfalls

THE VOYAGE to Hawaii was almost too easy. The Pacific can be like that—days of sailing through nothing bigger than four-foot swells and winds of fifteen knots. *Dove* behaved well and so did the kittens once they had gained their sea legs.

It was a relief to discover that the steering vane worked well and that I could move about the deck and the cabin confident that I was sailing within a few degrees of my course.

As the sun went down I began to feel sick, a new and surprising experience because I was a good sailor. I thought the symptoms were just reaction to the tension of getting away and to the first chill of loneliness.

Loneliness was to ride with me for a thousand days, and throughout the longest nights. At times it was like something I could touch. Loneliness slunk aboard as the lights of Catalina island began to fade, and I told myself that time and distance would destroy it. How wrong I was. There was no way of striking down this enemy, and my only defense was the business that a boat demands when under way, the activity called for by a sudden squall or the concentration of taking a fix on sun or stars.

At nine o'clock I forced myself to eat a can of stew and then tuned the radio to my favorite Los Angeles rock music station. It was interesting to hear the news announcer report that I was on my way—"the first schoolboy ever to attempt to sail the world alone." The announcer audaciously guessed a lot too, and guessed wrong when he added, "The most important piece of Robin's luggage is a shelf of schoolbooks."

"Like hell," I told the cats.

At dusk the sea was lit by phosphorescence, tiny flashlights in the folding water which moved away from the rudder. The phosphorescence reminded me of looking down at Los Angeles from an airliner at night. You see things differently when you are alone. The sea seemed to be putting on a special show for an audience of one. Even the stars seemed now to be for my own entertainment.

But into my tape recorder I spoke of simpler things: *Joliette has diarrhea. The kittens are not enthusiastic about the spray, which takes them by surprise as it comes over the bow. I have just dried them off with a hand towel and they've taken over my sleeping bag. Catalina almost out of sight. Wind a steady fifteen knots.*

If any one piece of additional equipment aboard *Dove* was more important than the rest it was my portable battery-operated tape recorder. With it I not only filled out the bare details entered in my logbook, but I recorded, sometimes too intimately, my fears and hopes, my passing thoughts and deepest feelings. Throughout the voyage at every port of call I mailed the tapes to my home. They make up about two hundred hours or more of listening—mostly unimportant, idle chatter, the names of men and places, sightings of fish, boats and aircraft. But when there was danger and excitement, the magnetic ribbon caught these too. Above the sound of my voice can be heard, at times, the roar and thunder of a storm or the squeaks of dolphins nuzzling *Dove's* hull.

On the second day out from San Pedro I recorded: *Made 103 miles in twenty-four hours, mostly under a reefed jib. Didn't sleep till dawn, then slept till ten. Kittens eating now, dancing and clawing at everything that moves. Breakfasted off eggs and* potatoes and a tuna sandwich. *Spray hit my sandwich as I was putting it into my mouth, so I didn't need to salt it.* I'm worried about the alcohol stove, which last night flared up for no reason. I'm also worried by the amount of kerosene my Coleman lamp is using.

At nightfall I had hung the Coleman aft so that its five hundred candlepower would bathe the cockpit and the sails with light and hopefully provide additional warning to shipping in my path. The lamp had to be pumped every two hours, a chore that soon wearied me.

On the afternoon of my third day at sea the sky clouded over. With the gloom my spirits dropped. Throughout my voyage I was to discover that weather affected my mood. Given a clear sky my morale was good—unless I was sitting in the doldrums. But when the sky was overcast I was often gloomy too and even minor problems worried me.

That third night I recorded: *Just had dinner of canned turkey and yams, which stuck to the roof of my mouth. I'll have to do something about my cooking! Took my first moon LOP* [line of position] *with a sextant.*

There followed several days of the kind of sailing that an elderly aunt would enjoy on a Sunday afternoon in San Pedro harbor— winds strong enough to fill the main and jib but not so strong as to put the gunwales under. From the start I had looked on this first leg to Hawaii as a shakedown cruise, a testing of *Dove's* response to wind and water, and of my skills as captain, navigator, mate and cook. Much time was taken up with sextant reading and checking LOPs with the dead reckoning of my taffrail log.

On the tenth day I hit the trades, which pushed Dove along 120 miles in twenty-four hours, and the clear night sky allowed me to take my first star fix. I was really excited about this and taped: *It's two o'clock in the morning and I know exactly where I am. That's kind of fun.*

When I'd been out sixteen days I picked up a Hawaiian radio station and introduced the cats to Hawaiian music. I complained into the recorder: *They don't seem to appreciate the music as much as I do. The Honolulu station has just spoken about me. The announcer read a letter from my father, who's asked all ships to look out for me. That's me they're talking about! They talked for five minutes, really weird! But I haven't seen any ships anyway. The only way I know that there are other people somewhere is by a jet trail. I'm trying to picture a guy sailing along in a small boat in the mid-Pacific. And that guy's me!*

All along my route I was to find out that the first or the second question a news reporter asked me was what I did all the time at sea. It sounds strange, but I was hardly ever without something to do—usually small things like cleaning up the boat, or mending something, or cooking. If there wasn't anything to do I'd read or make work, like painting the inside of the cabin or cleaning up the stove.

I would make quite a big deal out of writing a note and putting it into a bottle. The first time I did this was when I was on my way to Hawaii. The note read:

"My name is Robin Lee Graham. I am sixteen years old and sailing a 24 foot sailboat to Honolulu. My position is 127° W; 22° N. If you find this note please write to me and tell me where you found it. Thanks a lot." I added my uncle's California address. I never did receive a reply to my bottled notes. Perhaps they are still bobbing about in the Pacific or yellowing in the sun on some distant shore.

My library included Michener's *Hawaii* (which I enjoyed very much), Hiscock's *Beyond the West Horizon*, Steinbeck's *East of Eden*, Dana's *Two Years Before the Mast*, Heyerdahl's story of his Kon-Tiki voyage, Nordhoff and Hall's *Mutiny on the Bounty*. My schoolbooks remained under the used clothing in the cabin— although I was full of good intentions.

So these early days passed, with me writing my log, taking fixes with a sextant, feeding the cats, washing my clothes, always tidying up the boat. Generally I stayed awake at night and slept from dawn till perhaps midmorning. There were a few moments of alarm.

I told the tape recorder: *Gosh, I was scared. I mean, all this water sloshing about. I really thought Dove was sinking. What else? I was just about to blow up the life raft when I discovered what was wrong. One of the plastic fittings had melted—I suppose by the engine exhaust when I was charging the batteries. It was fantastic how quickly the water had come through. Anyway, I pumped out the bilge and made another plug out of a little piece of wood. Wow, man! Anyway, it's all okay now and we're scooting along at about four knots.*

Another question often asked me, at least in my first year of sailing, was what my parents thought about the voyage. Mother never hid her opposition and I believe she actually spoke to lawyers to try to stop my voyage. But Father was always for it. Shortly after he had seen me leave San Pedro, he wrote a letter to my mother to try to stop her from worrying, and he later published the letter in various newspapers, perhaps to answer all the criticism of my parents for allowing a schoolboy to face "not only the dangers of the deep," as one newspaper correspondent put it, "but the perils of the savages." Father's letter read:

Dearest Norma,

Our work is done and Lee has sailed. I watched the boat until it was out of sight in the morning mist. I returned to the slip to pick up some things. All the farewell wishers were gone. The slip was empty.

As I drove home without him sitting beside me as we had done for so many days I had a great big empty feeling. We have been so close and so busy, and now there is nothing. I feel Lee has sailed out of my life. I have lost his boyhood companionship. When I see him again he will be a man, looking for a life of his own with other friends and other interests where you and I are not included.

It happens to all parents, but it is so hard to take when it happens all of a sudden as it did to me, as he moved out of his slip and down the channel. I don't think I would ever have let him go if I didn't love him so much. It would have been easier on me to have kept him at home.

In my heart I know it is the right thing to let him go. He was happier today than I have ever seen him, or than he probably ever will be. And happier at sixteen than most people ever will be after living a comfortable life—stretching it to a safe end.

Lee knows the risk he is taking as he knows there are risks to those at home. Nobody can be entirely protected from the mishaps of life.

If anything should happen to Lee—and it would be the end of me if it did—I would still feel that I did the right thing for him.

Success or failure, he is fulfilling his destiny. We all have only one life, some are short and some are long. He loves life and wants a little more out of it than to follow convention out of fear of what others may think, or to be just another face in the crowd that follows the herd.

Please don't worry about Lee. The boat is as safe as can be. He knows this is the greatest thing that could happen to him and he appreciates what we have done for him to make it possible.

With love, Lyle

I am sure my father wrote that letter quite sincerely. I know he was really worried to see me go. But later, when he still wanted to control me from afar, I had to remind him that he had given me my freedom. I learned that our ideas of freedom were different because later there was to be much hurt to both of us.

Dove continued toward Hawaii at a steady pace, and I continued to record on tape the small happenings of my progress: *Cats pounced on a flying fish and look as contented as if they had eaten a jar of cream. . . . Today is Friday the thirteenth* [of August]. *Just took down the mainsail—not because of the date but because of a squall. Enjoyed seawater bath—poured buckets of brine over my head. Gosh, it's good to feel clean. . . . The smell in the cabin has disappeared, so it must have been me that caused it and not the cats. . . .*

August fifteenth and five o'clock A.M. *Wow! Just saw my first ship. . . . That boat reported me. Listening to my radio and heard over Honolulu radio that I have been sighted. The radio said that there had been "some anxiety about my safety." That's a lot of bull. Who could get into trouble in this kind of weather?*

Anyway, I was ahead of my ETA, because the ship had reported my position only 270 miles east northeast of Oahu.

Newspapers in California and Hawaii were having a field day. What they did not know they continued to guess. One paper, I was to read later, reported me "industriously working at my school-books." The paper added: "Hawaiian hospitality is famous but Robin Lee won't be attending all the parties he's been invited to because he's anxious to qualify for his high school diploma. He believes that the best way to learn is to get away to a quiet place —like the ocean."

So many newspapers wrote about me as if I were Little Lord Fauntleroy. Actually I had still not opened a schoolbook. I preferred fishing. My fishing equipment was in Honolulu, but I worked out my own method of changing my diet. One day I put a piece of canned tuna in a plastic bag and trailed it on a string. I gripped the other end of the string in my teeth so that my hands would be free to hold my bow and arrow. A big mahimahi came alongside, sniffed at the plastic bag and then snapped at it. I was lucky not to lose my front teeth and I didn't get the fish. At that moment a plane circled low overhead. An hour later my radio reported that my mother was aboard. They had been searching for me for an hour.

Easily the best moments of ocean sailing are those when land is first sighted. I saw Oahu at dawn on my twenty-second day at sea and whooped so loudly that the cats arched their backs. Outside Ala Wai harbor a Coast Guard power boat came alongside and offered a tow. With so many small boats around it seemed a good idea to accept.

The press and television must have been short of news. They came out of the harbor in a small armada. One of the reporters shouted across the water, "What are you going to do when you get ashore?"

"Find a men's room and take a shower," I said.

Actually I felt terribly tired as I tied up Dove at a slip close to the spot from where Jim and Art and I had sailed out in the ill-fated HIC. I had been forced to remain awake for the previous three nights as I had run out of kerosene for my Coleman lamp. I had taken no more than cat naps by day—perhaps fourteen hours' sleep in the previous sixty.

It was marvelous seeing my mother again and my brother Michael, and I didn't mind the pretty girls who necklaced me with leis. Hawaii is always fun. But I was anxious to be away again and to get out of range of people who gushed about my being the youngest solo sailor to make the California–Hawaii trip. A few days later my father flew over from California and helped me prepare Dove for the journey south.

Now I was moving into the big league. Dove and I had to be ready for anything that the sea could throw at us.

The only reason I spent as much as three weeks in Hawaii was that the inboard was causing trouble. It was a lousy engine to start with, worn and ill-used, and the spare parts did little to improve its efficiency. My father and I installed an additional outboard with an extension shaft. The outboard was light enough to be hauled up and lashed to the stern.

I sailed out of Ala Wai at noon on September 14, my destination Fanning island, a tiny speck of coral (actually twelve square miles) 1,050 miles almost due south. With fair winds I hoped to make Fanning in ten days, but in case my navigation slipped I took on provisions for sixty. In my wallet I had seventy dollars—not very much for a global voyager.

How much harder to say good-bye this time. What made it especially hard was that I knew how much my mother hated my going and how she really feared for me. It was difficult to meet her eyes, hidden behind a pair of dark glasses.

A strange woman in a muumuu near the slip began ringing a bell. I was not sure whether this was intended as a salute or a tocsin. Anyway, this time there were no storm warnings hoisted on the harbor wall.

Mother followed me out in a friend's launch. There were last farewells, final shouts of "Good luck" and "Happy landings" and "See you when you arrive." Then, following the old Hawaii custom, I threw my leis into the water. Hawaiians say that the traveler who does this will return to the islands again. The cats had been decorated with leis too. I forgot to throw their leis into the sea. The cats did not return to the islands.

Then *Dove* was away under a main and a blue and white genoa.

Two hours out of Hawaii I realized that I was not as brave as I had pretended. My throat was so tight it was hard to swallow. I told my tape recorder: *Sure hated to leave. Wondering if I'll ever see my parents again. I suppose saying good-bye always hurts. It can't hurt more than this. I seem to be traveling at only one knot. But at least I'm pointing in the right direction. How long will it take me to sail around the world at this speed? Cats look miserable too. Oh, God, I'm so homesick!*

I was not a bit hungry, but I had to do something to stop my misery—to stop me from crying in fact. I made a spaghetti dinner and over my shoulder I watched the glow of Honolulu begin to fade. Fortunately, at the moment when I was just about to break down completely, a squall raced out of the northeast and *Dove* picked up to four knots. The last lights of Oahu disappeared quickly over the horizon.

It took *Dove* four days to reach the trades and then the water turned a glorious turquoise blue—the kind of water that tempts you to jump over the side for a swim.

Even wearing a harness—and there were very rare moments when I took it off at sea—to jump over the side would have been crazy, because if there had been a sudden puff of wind I probably would not have been able to haul myself back on board.

Only four days out of Hawaii I saw the most beautiful sunset of the whole five years of my voyage. At least that is the one I best remember. I took a picture of it, but it doesn't really show up well. There was no one to point it out to except the cats, and they weren't interested, so I told the tape: *The reds and the pinks are* sort of coming toward me from the horizon and then the greens and the yellows are moving in and out like they're being woven.

I needed something like this to cheer me up because I was still so homesick. Loneliness slowed me down. When my morale was low I spent much longer calculating my position and making entries in my logbook.

On days when the cats irritated me I complained into the tape recorder: *Suzette and Joliette are so dumb. Why can't they talk back to me? All they can do is chase their tails and go to sleep. . . . I don't know what's wrong. I don't even want to eat. Even that fruitcake you gave me tastes like warm water. You know what I mean?*

It was weird how when I was on the skids of self-pity something would turn up to distract me. The sunset was one example, and another was when I was in the doldrums under flopping sails, twelve days out from Hawaii: I saw my first school of porpoises.

I recorded: *The porpoises are now all around Dove. I can hear their squeaks. It's amazing how loud they can talk. I guess I can hear them so well because my hull is so thin. I wonder if they're trying to talk to me. Maybe one porpoise hit the keel, because I heard a thumping and she was squeaking real loud. It was nerve-racking but exciting. It has been so long since I heard any voice, and it's almost as though someone was trying to answer me.*

To celebrate the visit of the porpoises I gave the cats a sardine supper.

At times I was quite desperate to hear a human voice. Sometimes I would talk into the tape for a while and just play it back. I'd hear myself say: *Everything okay here, but what's happening at home? What? I can't hear you. Why don't you answer me? Are you sulking or something? Ah, well, if you won't talk to me I'll just have to go on talking to myself. Now this is my routine. I get up and put my sleeping bag away. Then I comb my hair as if a girl was coming to breakfast. Wish she was. Some seaweed just passing the boat. First I've seen. I'm overcooking my hard-boiled eggs. Perhaps six minutes should do them properly. Seventy-six-*

mile run in the past twenty-four hours. That's a little better. Woke up last night and found I was going due north. How long did I go the wrong way? Squall probably turned me around. I have to wake up regularly in the night to check my course and set the sails and pump up the lamp. Reading a book called High Wind in Jamaica. More porpoises came alongside. I paid no attention to them. They seemed to resent that. They began to squeak at me—real high squeaks. They seemed to be saying, "Look at me. We'll race you to the next seaweed." They'd win every time. Going to have tuna and yams for dinner.

I was beginning to pick up the lore of the sea, learning to read the clouds, watching the drift of seaweed, marking the movement of the wind. Even my cooking improved. I discovered the best timing for a hard-boiled egg and how much water to add to hot cereal. I developed, too, a special understanding of sound. Even asleep I could sense a change in the wind or sea conditions.

My mother once told me that she could hear a baby's cry in a thunderstorm. The weird way I could hear the sounds of the sea, the wind and the boat, even when asleep, saved me much time and hundreds of miles, and more than once saved my life. Alerted by a change in wave patterns, I would immediately awaken, sometimes to find Dove pushed off course by a veering wind.

Most of the time Joliette and Suzette were good company and I gave them a good report on the tape: It's fun to watch them find their sea legs. They've learned how to bend their legs and lean over to keep their balance. They don't like the hot weather, though. When it's really hot I wrap them in damp towels. They seem to appreciate this. Then when the sun moves over and it gets cooler they creep out and start to play with each other. Both the cats love to watch the water when it runs along the gunwales. They sit absolutely still as if they are waiting to pounce on a mouse or something.

When I'd figured out that I was about fifty miles from Fanning I became really uptight. I taped: I'm somewhere close to the island. I'm sure of that. But where is it? Pity there aren't any milestones in the sea. My eyes are searching the horizon. I'm beginning to wonder if I've missed this first landfall. . . . Every few minutes I stand on the cabin roof but there's not a bump on the horizon. Oh, gosh, supposing I'm south of Fanning! It sounds crazy, but I'm beginning to look astern. That shows I don't trust myself too much.

Then suddenly I saw it. *Land! Land!* I yelled into the recorder. Then turning to Joliette I said: *Don't you see it, you fool? Out there, five points starboard of the bow!*

I had been alone two weeks with no single sign of human life, no ship, no plane, no jet trail, not even a floating beer can. The sight of Fanning, still a tiny nipple, made me half crazy with excitement.

As the island grew bigger and I began to see the darker shadows of vegetation, I smugly told the tape: *Robin Lee Graham, you're a pretty good navigator.*

I reached English harbor at five in the afternoon of September 29. A white man in a diesel boat came out and threw me a line. When *Dove* was tied up to a small stone jetty in six feet of water, I climbed the steps. The pilot put out his hand and said his name was Phillip Palmer.

"Welcome," he said. "We don't get many visitors."

Just hearing a human voice again was weird. Sure I had listened to the radio, but a voice over the radio is always neutral and bloodless. Mr. Palmer's voice was warm and friendly. What embarrassed me was how inarticulate I had become. My thoughts seemed ten paces ahead of my tongue, but if Mr. Palmer believed me to be mentally retarded he was too polite to show it.

The only European on the island, he was a grizzled fellow who supervised three hundred natives, imported from the Gilbert islands to harvest profitable copra crops for the Burns Philip Company. Mr. Palmer was not only harbor master and labor manager, but wore half a dozen other hats. He would settle disputes, regulate supplies, operate communications and, if necessary, set a broken limb. He was also a kindly host.

I accepted his invitation to sleep in his little house, to have supper with him and breakfast too. The food was prepared by his native housekeeper, Marybell. Her meals reminded me what a bad cook I was. In his beat-up Volkswagen Mr. Palmer drove me around the island to watch native dancing. Fanning is an angler's paradise; a huge variety of fish, both in the harbor and in inland pools, seemed to want to commit suicide. I could almost hook them on my toenails. The harbor was like a huge aquarium.

Fanning's local name means "Footprint of Heaven." The island is beautiful, and I guess from above it looks like a human foot. Visitors are as rare as rich uncles so I was given VIP treatment. The children at the local school put on a special dance for me. The dancers later invited me to join them in a sort of wild fandango and then, on Sunday, they invited me to their little church. It was weird for a California pagan to hear himself prayed for in the Gilbertine language. But it meant quite a lot to me that these childlike people should ask God to give me safe sailing to wherever I wanted to go.

I spent six days on Fanning, refilled my tanks with spring water, took on fresh eggs, a terrific bread made with coconut milk and a few souvenirs, including a hand-carved model canoe. My visit to the island cost me exactly twenty cents—one dime and two nickels which fell out of my pocket when I joined the children's dance. When I left I gave a sweater to kindly Marybell and a Mickey Mouse T-shirt to her little boy who was sick.

Mr. Palmer refused to take any money from me when I gave him a radiogram to be sent to my parents in Hawaii. I was two days out of Fanning when I remembered I had forgotten to give Mr. Palmer my proper home address. This meant that my parents would not know where I was, and I was so mad that I kicked myself half across Dove's deck. I never realized though that my long silence would cause huge headlines in Hawaii and California.

Several weeks later I received a bundle of American newspapers. In inch-high type the *Los Angeles Herald-Examiner* had told its readers: "BOY WORLD SAILOR IS MISSING," and the *Honolulu Star-*

Bulletin carried a three-column story headlined: "MOTHER OF ISLE BOY NOT ALARMED AT NO WORD."

For two weeks the oldest members at the Ala Wai Yacht Club shook their heads, remembering the *HIC* episode as they read daily reports, each more pessimistic than the last, that the "teenage world sailor was long overdue."

Meanwhile I was sailing on under jib and genoa, wing and wing, to Pago Pago, and since I carried a bag of mail for Mr. Palmer, *Dove* could have flown a Royal Mail pennant on her mast.

I guess it was a conscience pricked by my forgetfulness that made me open my schoolbooks for the first time. With the self-steering gear in operation, I finished part one of my American literature course, reading the lives of Captain John Smith and Benjamin Franklin. (*Quite interesting really*, I told the tape.)

Time for study was no big problem when *Dove* wallowed in the doldrums, and south of Fanning I sailed mostly in light airs. When the occasional winds filled the sails they usually came from the wrong direction. I protested into the tape recorder: *The wind blows from all sides. I've never had it blow the way it's supposed to. The wind is really messed up. It's not supposed to do this at all. It's just not in the books.*

On October 7 *Dove* rolled slowly over the equator and I wrote in my logbook: *Cats are now officially shellbacks.* It was too hot for celebrations, although one Hawaiian reporter recorded later that I had "doubtless dubbed the cats' paws with peanut butter."

At one point I thought I'd gone crazy and that my memory had left me. Someone at Honolulu had given me a cup and ball game, and when tidying up the cabin I found it under the pillow on the quarter bunk. I was absolutely sure that I had parked it on a cabin shelf. Anyway, I put it back in place. Ten minutes later I went below again and found the game under the same pillow. I was really scared. It was weird because obviously there was no one else aboard. A second time I returned the game to the shelf and went back to the cockpit. Then a slight thump inside the cabin disturbed me. It was Suzette. I caught her red-handed. She was pulling the game from the shelf and hiding it under my pillow. I was so relieved to know I wasn't completely off my rocker that I didn't punish her—at least not until she discovered my Fanning eggs.

Mentally I was in poor shape, worried not only by the slowness of my doldrums progress but because I knew my family would soon be thinking that disaster was the only explanation for my long silence.

A head shrinker would have marked the symptoms. On my sixth day out of Fanning I burst into tears just because I failed to make a milk pudding taste even remotely like the kind my mother made.

Strangely I wasn't as worried by more serious setbacks, like when a shark gobbled up my taffrail-log spinner, trailing twenty feet astern.

I happen to hate sharks. When the five-footer finned at my stern I shot him with my .22 pistol. The brute opened his mouth in surprise, showing teeth that looked as if they could snap a telephone pole. He thrashed wildly with his tail and then slowly keeled over and sank. Then I wondered why my taffrail line was floating on the surface. The shark had bitten the spinner clean off. I had no spare, so from then I had to guess how far I had traveled each day.

Anyway, the sea looked healthy, and I noted on the recorder: *Dove is now slicing through sheets of blue plankton and schools of small fish. Some of the fish are only about an inch or two long. It's weird how they keep pace with Dove for hours, even when I pick up a breeze and we scoot along at three or four knots. But I wonder why the decks are so dirty. I'm always having to clean them up and it's not the cats' fault. The cats are pretty good about using their litter box. Maybe those stinking cities are sending out their smog this far.*

On my fifteenth day out of Fanning I spotted land and my morale shot way up. My voice an octave higher on the tape, I reported: *I see it, I see it! It's right there. It's a kind of dome-shaped thing, but it's land. It's all rainy looking.* I had raised Tutuila, the main island of American Samoa.

To the nonsailor, navigation may seem like witchcraft, but really it's not at all difficult. The sextant is the key to it all. With this instrument I measure the altitude above the horizon of the sun, moon or stars, then mark the time to the second on my chronometer. After that it's simply a matter of looking up the nautical tables, making additions and subtractions which wouldn't strain an average ten-year-old and pinpointing my exact position on the charts.

That's the theory. In practice mistakes can be made. A faulty sextant or chronometer can throw out the result by many miles. The tiny island of Fanning, for example, surrounded by hundreds of miles of water, could easily be missed through careless calculations or a faulty sextant. Missing a landfall in a vast expanse of water could mean death.

There was no special reason for me to fear missing Samoa, because I was as used to a sextant as a doctor is to his stethoscope. Besides, I had the advantage on sailors of the days before radio because I could check my chronometer against radio signals. But I never quite trusted my navigation, and always had a feeling of achievement when I made my ports.

Perhaps it was because I was too pleased with myself on this occasion or because I was pushing Dove a little too hard that the accident happened. Dove was closing on Samoa when a squall hit, not a heavy squall but blustery enough to be taken seriously. The upshot was that the lower aft shroud broke. Within an eyeblink the mast buckled and fell overboard, carrying with it the mainsail and the jib. Although the wind was perhaps twenty knots, Dove stopped like a duck full of buckshot.

I told the tape: Here I was within fifteen miles of Tutuila after five hundred hours of sailing and now I'm not going to make it.

It took me twenty minutes to heave the sodden sails and broken mast aboard and two hours to raise the boom and set a jury rig with half the mainsail. I was in no great danger, but it seemed a good idea to put out the brilliant orange distress signal. When an aircraft headed my way I lit a flare, but aimed it at my bare right foot. The steam came off my toes as the aircraft headed out to sea.

Now, with the jury rig I could only sail downwind. A look at the chart and I saw that my only hope of an early landfall was to make for Apia on Upolu island, fifty-two miles distant.

A jet pilot once told me that he was trained for emergencies. A child, he claimed, could fly an airliner but what separated the men from the boys in the cockpit was the moment that might never happen in a long career—the moment when all the red lights start blinking. It's the same with sailing. Anyone can learn in half an afternoon to sail around a harbor, but an emergency like a demasting calls for seamanship. I was wondering just how good my seamanship was as the wind drove crippled *Dove* under her clumsy shortened sail toward Upolu's jagged lee shore.

Due more to a lucky shift of wind than to my sailing skill, *Dove* nosed past Danger Point. At dawn next morning sandy beaches were on my beam and green hills beyond. I celebrated with a breakfast of canned asparagus. By noon I had anchored in the lovely harbor of Apia, right opposite Aggie's Hotel.

After going through customs, my first duty ashore was to deliver Mr. Palmer's mailbag and then to send a cable to my parents—rightly addressed this time. My next worry was to find someone to mend an aluminum mast.

It would be five months before I could safely sail again.

The delay at Apia didn't really worry me because the hurricane season was approaching and I was in no hurry to leave. In the harbor the rusted wreck of a German warship, the *Adler*, which went down in a hurricane in 1889, was a daily reminder of what hurricanes can do to craft much bigger than *Dove*. Besides, Upolu, the chief isle of Western Samoa, is really nice and I didn't plan on being a typical tourist and "doing" Upolu in five days.

It was important to me, from the moment I set out from California, to get to know the people in distant places, to understand their customs and their life styles, to eat their foods, to bargain in their markets, to listen to their music and to learn their folklore.

First impressions of Apia were encouraging. Lovely Polynesian girls in vivid costumes looked like butterflies as they walked the streets. At Aggie's famous hotel two of these girls beat a wooden gong at mealtimes to summon guests to the dining room. Aggie Grey, half New Zealander, half Polynesian, the founder-owner of the hotel, had read about me in some newspaper. She invited me to be her tariff-free table guest for as long as I cared to stay.

Joshua Slocum, the first American to sail alone around the world, had had a cooler reception at Apia in 1896. The islanders had refused to believe that Slocum could have crossed the Pacific without help and they angrily accused him of eating his crew.

Aggie's son, Alan, became my friend and introduced me to Sam Heywood, principal of the local technical school, who said he could mend Dove's mast. Mr. Heywood took a lot of trouble welding the jagged mast ends together and then pushing a hardwood core up the hollow to the weld. The mistake we made was when we stepped it. I forgot the sailor's superstition that a coin should be put at the mast's base—a mistake I was later to remember and regret.

Another stupid thing I did at Apia was to claim I'd shot the shark with my bow and arrow. I lied because I thought that the possession of a gun would cause me trouble with the port officials. Of course the bow and arrow story was told at the bars and I felt pretty silly.

Polynesian food is the best in the world. Anyone who challenges this claim can meet me across a table groaning under roasted pig basted in coconut milk, taro, breadfruit and papaya.

As with all the islands, Upolu is full of legends. The one that I especially liked was about the origin of the coconut tree. The islanders tell the story of a girl named Sina whose beauty was reported to a Fijian king. So fascinated was the king that he decided to marry Sina. To help him win her he changed himself into an eel and swam to Upolu. The eel became Sina's special pet, but when it began to make passes at her she understandably got frightened and fled. The fable has its variations, but essentially the eel is said to have chased Sina from island to island until he was worn out. In his last breath the eel confessed his love to Sina and that he was really a king. The eel promised that if Sina would bury him in front of her Upolu home he would always provide her with shade, food and drink. So Sina watched a snakelike plant grow out of the grove, watched it throw out shade-giving fronds and strange fruit. This was, of course, the coconut tree, and every time Sina drank from its fruit she knew she was kissing her royal lover.

One of my first expeditions at Apia was a visit to the tomb of Robert Louis Stevenson, who, like Gauguin in Tahiti, had become a legend in his time. The tomb is quite high up on Mount Vaea, overlooking the town. I could have driven there by way of the tree-lined "Road of Loving Hearts" built by the people of Samoa for their beloved Tusitala ("Teller of Tales"), but I preferred to climb the five-hundred-foot trail up the face of the hill. In the early morning light I read the Requiem carved on the stone tomb:

> Home is the sailor, home from the sea,
> And the hunter home from the hill.

My guide told me how the Scots author had come to Upolu in 1890 for the sake of his health and how the islanders really loved him. Stevenson's big Victorian home nearby is now a museum.

I was given an outrigger canoe and paddled to and from Dove every night and morning. One midnight I was awakened by one of the cats crying and found Joliette looking over Dove's side. Suzette had fallen overboard and was thrashing about in the water. I fished her out and dried her. She would certainly have drowned if Joliette had not sounded the alarm.

On another occasion when I returned to Dove in the outrigger I found Suzette clinging to the anchor chain. She was just waiting for me to rescue her.

I don't know whether it was because of something I ate, or what, but suddenly I broke out in boils. They continued to worry me for a year. I went to find medical help and learned that Western Samoan doctors, some unqualified, have a reputation in the islands for healing people. One unqualified doctor discovered, for instance, that the juice of the coconut is quite sterile and that coconut fibers are as good as catgut for sewing up wounds. I was told that when they ran out of gut in World War II, some GIs had their wounds sewn up with coconut fibers. It seems that the Fijian eel king gave Sina more gifts than she recognized.

My first Christmas away from home was really quite cheerful. I exchanged gifts with Aggie and Alan, and received from home parcels containing a plastic spare sextant, more recording tapes, a new taffrail-log spinner, heavy-duty shrouds and a Gibson Girl radio—a transmitter that would allow me to send out distress signals.

A few days before I was due to leave Upolu a young lawyer from Pago Pago, George Wray, invited me to climb Mount Matavanu on the nearby island of Savaii. The mountain rises above a plateau to its volcanic mouth, which occasionally growls. George believed that it had never been climbed. We set out together at dawn, mosquito nets and bedrolls on our backs, and we climbed for twelve hours. Our progress was very slow because of tough ferns and high trees. Every now and then we would break through the ferns and trees and find ourselves in beautiful meadows filled with wild flowers—perfect places for homesteading or for a Robinson Crusoe. When the sun went down George and I slept on the ferns and the silence was weird.

In the little fishing village below they had told us stories of beautiful women who wandered about the mountainside at night but whose kisses were as cold as the mist. We saw no women, fleshed or otherwise, but imagination can work overtime in such places. We had to return the following morning without making the summit because George was scheduled to defend a man in court in Pago Pago.

Climbing down this quiet, weird mountain was harder than going up. Eventually we followed a stream, which became a cascade every few hundred yards. When working our way around one of these cascades George slipped. I was luckily able to grab him, because he would probably have broken a leg on the jagged volcanic rocks.

George really knew his plants and trees. He showed me a jungle vine that provided a thirst-quenching drink. When the vine was slashed near its base it sizzled and hissed for a few seconds like a boiling kettle, and then a liquid poured out as if from a faucet. The liquid had a slight sawdust flavor but was quite refreshing.

As it was the first time I had worn shoes since leaving California, my feet were badly blistered. I was close to dropping when we heard voices. The missionary at the coast had sent out a search party of small boys. It was good to see these grinning Polynesian boys, who led us back to their mission. I gave them my tennis shoes, bush knife, mosquito net and my spare pair of Levi's.

On January 3, 1966, I left Apia for Pago Pago, and I had just got outside the harbor when a tropical squall tested Dove's repaired mast and rigging. The squall didn't last for long and I told the tape: Now it's going to be a lovely sail. The wind is coming out of the southwest. I feel much better equipped for the sea. Trying out my new plastic sextant. It was hard to say good-bye to Aggie and Alan. They've been real nice to me. . . . Heading straight for Pago Pago. Some porpoises have just come up and said hello. They seem to be welcoming me back to the sea again.

～ 3

Where Earth Day Begins

It was a two-day sail to Pago Pago (pronounced Pango Pango), chief town and port of American Samoa. I was back in civilization and not liking it too well. The islands boast six television stations, luxury hotels, a jet airport and a bus service that almost keeps to its timetable.

Several ocean-cruising yachts were in the harbor. There is a comradeship among yachtsmen in a foreign port, a comradeship created by common experiences. Sailing in the South Seas brings out the best in people. They become warm, free and friendly. Parties aboard are fun, the talk sincere—not the phony talk often heard in the suburban lounge and country club.

Later I was to meet in their home environments a number of yachtsmen I had known at sea. The Jekyll and Hyde transformation was weird. The fellow who had laughed in Polynesia and who was ready to lend you a jib or a jar of pickles could become cold, aloof, suspicious of real friendship as soon as he walked the soft carpets of his home. And when his wife changed her salt-stained jeans for a cocktail dress she too often reverted to another personality—not the kind I liked.

Not every yachtsman changes back to what he was before he sailed. Some carry with them to their homes and to Main Street the spell of the islands, the honesty and fun of the islanders.

It was still the hurricane season, and it seemed a good idea to hole up in Pago Pago. As it turned out, *Dove*, riding at anchor in the harbor, came through the worst hurricane to hit Samoa in seventy years.

On January 29, in the early afternoon, a port official rowed past *Dove* and shouted, "Batten down. She's on her way."

The barometer was dropping fast, so I took down the wind vane, lashed the sails, removed the awning and put out extra mooring lines. My California friend, Jud Croft, who had flown to Samoa a few weeks earlier, joined me aboard *Dove*.

Sunset was red, ugly, ominous, and a gusty wind began to whip up the harbor water. The barometer continued to drop, falling from 29.70 to 29.20 in a few hours. Two oceangoing yachts scuttled into harbor as if the devil were at their heels. Down in *Dove*'s snug cabin Jud and I watched the mounting drama through the portholes. We were excited, the way you feel when you know something big is going to happen. I turned on my tape recorder to give a running commentary:

Nine o'clock at night. Gusts of wind are hurling spray through the air like snow in a blizzard. . . . Dove swinging and rolling from gunwale to gunwale. . . . Ten o'clock. Man, I never imagined there could be wind like this. . . . Through the ports I can see the lights going out in the town—whole streets suddenly blackened as the power fails or telephone poles crash. . . . Radio says full force of hurricane won't hit till midnight. . . . But here we go! Hold on! Wow! That blast dipped the port gunwale under water. . . . Midnight . . . Noise now unbelievable. Radio says winds are topping one hundred miles an hour. . . . The boat—no! I can't believe it! The wind is picking her up and throwing her on her side until the ports are covered. Imagine that! No sails, just bare poles. . . . Sea pouring over cockpit combing. This is really swinging, man! Ports have gone right under. . . . Boy, my ears are popping. . . . Suzette and Joliette keeping their cool. Guess they know they have nine lives. . . . On the shore I can just make out palm trees kissing the ground—looking like sea urchins when the tide goes out. . . . Wow! I thought that was it! We heeled over eighty-five degrees.

In the replay Jud and I can be heard screaming, yelling with laughter and exhilaration. Nature provides nothing to match a hurricane—devastating though it always is—for sheer thrill which tightens the nerves like violin strings. It was a fantastic night.

Winds began to ease before dawn, but the radio reported some gusts went off the scale. The yacht *Marinero* with a crew of three whom I'd recently gotten to know was missing. Several days later parts of the *Marinero* wreck were found—but not the bodies of my friends.

Next morning I looked over *Dove* for damage. There was almost none. A small section of the jib had been torn free from the lashing and had shredded.

On the island it was a different story. Armed with cameras, Jud and I hitchhiked along rubble-strewn roads to the village of Tula, which had taken the worst of the storm. Half the village had been blown away.

Most native houses in Samoa are lightly constructed and cheap to replace. At Tula we found neighbor helping neighbor to clear the debris and to build new homes. Jud and I joined the clean-up force and the islanders seemed grateful. A Polynesian lady, Mrs. Fa'ava Pritchard, invited us to dinner and to spend the night in her home, which had survived because it was one of the few built of concrete blocks. We talked a lot about the hurricane and exchanged stories of escapes, and then Mrs. Pritchard asked me what I was doing. I told her about *Dove*.

When I had finished she nodded her head and was silent for a moment. Then she said, "I'm giving you a new name. You are Lupe Lele. In our language that means 'Flying Dove.'"

I was quite touched. After dinner they turned on the radio to a local rock station and the old grandmother asked me to dance with her. Her face was as wrinkled as a walnut but she outdanced me.

Next morning Mrs. Pritchard taught me how to make banana pancakes with my fingers. I've forgotten how much flour she used, but I remember the rest of the recipe. Mash up ten bananas into a creamy paste, add three teaspoons of sugar, three cups of sour milk, one cup of water and stir well. The mixture is then fried in hot oil until brown. Finally each pancake is dipped like a doughnut in sugar and served with fresh fruit. This makes a breakfast for a Samoan family of five. I recommend it.

Pago Pago is one of the busiest ports in the South Seas and is visited by a variety of ships of many nationalities. An anchored Russian freighter especially intrigued me because the Coast Guard patrolled it twenty-four hours a day, and the port people treated the crew unkindly. I talked to a couple of the crew and they invited me aboard. When I gave the men a bag of coconuts they pressed some evil-looking cigarettes into my hand. A third crew member, who spoke broken English, handed me a pamphlet, promising me several times over that it was "not political." I cannot vouch for that because I lost the pamphlet before I'd had a chance to read it. I was sorry for the crew, though, because they seemed to be so controlled and did not appear to have much fun— and the Samoan islands are made for fun.

One evening when I returned to *Dove*, Suzette was missing. Earlier I had tied up to a wharf and the cats went wild as they rediscovered the smell and feel of earth and grass. A raffish-looking tomcat was working his way through trashcans, and I suspected pretty Suzette had been rapidly seduced. I never saw her again and missed her more than I cared to admit. When her sister was gone, Joliette stuck close to my heels, but she must also have had her night, because a few weeks later it became very obvious she was going to have kittens.

On May 1, after too long on land, I left Pago Pago for the Vavau group, a cluster of two hundred islands, some only a few yards across, of overwhelming variety. It was a good sail, through blustery winds and heavy seas, the kind of weather to test my seamanship once more. After four days I anchored *Dove* in Neiafu's harbor, which was cluttered with inter-island craft—a picture of masts, furled canvas and rolling sailors. I could have believed I was in Boston at the time of the Tea Party.

As I set foot ashore an old man came up to me and, taking off his hat, invited me to meet his friend Chief Kaho. I replied that what I wanted to do immediately was to charge *Dove's* batteries, so he said he would help me do this.

I wondered why these islanders were so friendly, and at first thought it was because I was young. But soon I was to learn that Tongans extend Polynesian hospitality to all *palalangi* (the name they give to foreigners, because it was the name they gave to the first white settlers). Explorer James Cook had well logged the archipelago the "Friendly Islands."

On the evening of my arrival I taped: *This must be one of the loveliest spots on all the earth. It is easy to understand why Chief Kaho said to me, "You will be happy here until the end of the world." My only complaint is that I ate too much of his lobster.*

After exploring some of the islands over the next few days, I told my tape recorder: *How different they are, these islands, different as flowers from flowers, trees from trees. People are too. Why do we lump people all together?*

The weather was marvelous and I cruised around the tiny islets and coral reefs of the southern part of the Vavau group. When the wind died completely I used my outboard, and in water as smooth and as clear as glass I dived and explored the marine life. The colors of some of the fish were unbelievable as they swam among the coral fronds. It was a new world down there, and it provided me with food too. I often found shells and began my collection, which in time was to grow quite large. I boiled the meat from the shells and soon learned which made the best meals.

In these islands and in other islands I visited some of the natives seemed to have a way of communicating with sharks and turtles. I was told of a ceremony at which the women actually call up the "mother of turtles," a huge creature said to be several hundred years old.

In the marketplaces on the bigger islands I bartered a few pieces of used clothing for mottled cowrie shells, handmade necklaces and fascinating tapa cloth. The cloth is made from beating out tree bark, drying it and painting it with geometric designs.

In the Vavau group I attended my first of several ritualistic kava ceremonies. Kava, a slightly narcotic drink, is the "coffee" of the islanders. It is made from the root of a pepper shrub and has a slight earthy flavor which I never really liked. If I drank a cup or two it simply dulled my tongue and lips as if I had had a light injection of Novocain. When I drank a gallon my legs seemed to be not quite my own. Many shops and offices keep kava bowls permanently filled. Kava is drunk by customers and staff in the way that Americans use office water fountains.

I was invited to a birthday party and sampled octopus, a special Tongan delicacy. My host told me why the fishermen go hunting octopus with rat-shaped lures.

Long ago, the legend goes, some birds, a hermit crab and a rat went canoeing, but a jealous kingfisher left out of the party pecked a hole in the boat. As the canoe began to sink, the birds flew away, the crab swam ashore but the drowning rat was saved by an octopus. Reaching the beach, the rat deliberately pissed on the octopus, which was naturally pretty upset. From the day of this insult octopuses look upon rats as their mortal foes. So Tongan fishermen still profitably exploit the ancient feud.

The gentleness of these people reaches into their language and I could sit for hours on a wharf or at a kava ceremony and just listen to the conversation. Almost every dialogue, even with a policeman, ends with the greeting "Mal e lelei, mal e folau" ("Good day, and thanks for coming").

It is not uncommon in the islands to give special names to visitors, and at a party in the Tongatabu group Chief Kalaniuvalu dubbed me Kai Vai.

"That means 'Eat Water,'" he said, and when I raised my eyebrows he laughed and added, "Now don't please be offended. It is the name given to the warrior in the prow of a boat, the warrior who protects his chief from spray. It is a name of honor."

At Nukualofa I was invited to the special *kili-kili* ceremony which marked the end of six months' mourning for the beloved Queen Salote, who had ruled Tonga for nearly half a century. The memorial rites lasted three days, during which the chiefs and elders covered the queen's tomb with thousands of gleaming volcanic stones collected mostly from Tofua island, about one hundred miles to the north.

My Tongan hostess loaned me a black costume and a *taovala*— a mat of plaited grass worn round the waist. At the ceremony at the "Abode of Love" I saw the new king, Taufaahau Tupou IV, but did not meet him. Although he weighs 350 pounds he is one of Tonga's best surfers and scuba divers.

The Tongans are a very religious people, and as their islands are close to the international date line they proudly claim that "This is where the new earth day begins, and so we are the first people in the world to pray each morning."

It was as hard for me to leave the Tongatabu group as it had been for Captain Cook two centuries before. I used Cook's own words to enter in my logbook:

"Thus we took leave of the Friendly Islands and their inhabitants after a stay of between two and three months, during which time we lived together in most cordial friendship."

On June 21 I set sail for Fulanga, ·in the Lau group, 210 miles away, in company with the yachts *Corsair II* from South Africa and *Morea* from California. Fulanga is an isolated atoll with bleached white beaches and a village of grass huts, as old as time. I traded ballpoint pens and clothing for carved kava bowls and tapa mats. Two days later *Dove* and the other two yachts put out for Suva, the busy port of the main island of the Viti Levu group, and the Fijian capital.

We had hardly passed Fulanga's northernmost land point when we were struck by a heavy sea and had to beat into the wind. As *Dove* was taking plenty of water, it seemed sensible to fall into the lee of Kambara island and wait for the weather to improve. I tried to signal my intention to the other yachts, but *Morea*, a sleek forty-three-footer, had already pulled ahead. I waved vigorously to Corsair's skipper, Stanley ("Jeff") Jeffrey, but he mistook my flailing arms for a friendly salute. He waved back cheerfully and sailed on.

The other yachts made Suva, assuming I was on their tail, but when after a couple of days I still had not arrived, they feared I had foundered. Jeff Jeffrey arranged for a radio alert.

I took my time, laying over for two days at Kambara island, where I was asked to take a sick woman to Suva. At the last moment the woman's family looked over Dove and shook their heads. I guess they decided that the sick woman would have a better chance of surviving if she stayed at home. So I sailed on with Joliette, now quite recovered from the birth of her stillborn kittens.

Under a full moon on July 2 I anchored Dove near Corsair and Morea in the harbor of Suva, the queen of the South Sea ports, and next morning went ashore. Here was an outpost of the British Empire, and I expected typical British hospitality. But a newly appointed Fijian port official pompously demanded a bond of one hundred dollars. I turned over the cash in my pocket. It amounted to exactly $23.43. Fortunately the American consul, who had apparently heard of me, came to my rescue by giving a guarantee that the U.S. government would grubstake me if I was stranded.

The local yacht club was a tourist center and Dove became a special exhibit. There was no escape for me, even in the cabin, because tourists peered through the portholes as if I were a new marine creature shipped in for the Harbor Light aquarium. The situation was not improved when the local paper talked about a "kid who had sailed the Pacific in a teacup."

The Fijians themselves are a handsome race, the men generally well muscled and towering over my five feet eight inches. They are true Melanesians, with very dark skins and frizzy upstanding hair that pleases them so much that it used to be a mortal offense even to touch a Fijian head. The Fijians are now outnumbered by the Indians, who first came to the islands as indentured labor in the last century and now control most of the commerce. Here, as on other islands which stretch from the Pacific to the African coast, there is considerable hostility and tension between the easygoing natives and the shrewd, hard-working immigrants from India.

For a few coins old men are ready to talk to tourists about the days when their forebears cooked *mbokola* (human flesh) by boiling it or by baking it in underground ovens. But the Fijians off the tourist paths do not like to be asked the flavor of missionaries. A taunt that can provoke a Fijian to fight is "*Kana nai vava Baker*" ("Eat the boots of Mr. Baker"), referring to the Reverend Thomas Baker, who was boiled at the last cannibal feast in 1867.

While I was at the main Fijian island I had the chance to explore the interior with a family friend from Hawaii, Mrs. Louise Meyer, skipper of another oceangoing yacht. Mrs. Meyer rented three horses and five of us took turns riding. The mounts were so scrawny that I preferred to walk. In the heart of the island we attended a Fijian kava ceremony which differed from the ones I had attended in Tongatabu.

Here the kava (called *yaqona*) was prepared by women, one of whom placed the ground root in a bowl and ritually added water from a segment of bamboo. The chief brewer pounded the root to a thin paste the color of mud, then strained it through the fibers of a hibiscus plant. Meanwhile the men chanted and clapped rhythmically and beat on a *lali*, a hollow wooden drum. The cupbearer received the drink in a coconut shell and then handed it to each of us in turn. The idea was to drain the cup in one draft and to shout "*Maca!*" ("It is finished!")

When the kava was gone, the local Fijians began a native dance with four bare-chested men beating a tattoo on their *lalis* and singing a ballad about the devil circling the world faster than an astronaut, with stopovers at New York, Cape Town and elsewhere. Although Christianized, the Fijians still like their ancient superstitions in which the devil plays a leading role along with soothsayers, sorcerers and the like.

Up to now on my voyage, when short of funds I had successfully bargained for food with my supply of used clothing and ballpoint pens. In Samoa and among the Tongans the bargaining had been a game, its rules unwritten but played with humor. In Fiji the response was altogether different. Attempts to trade seemed to bring out greed and cunning, a surliness suggesting that I had taken advantage of the vendors.

I spoke of this problem to a yachtsman friend, Dick Johnston, who had spent a lot of time among the Fijians and knew their language. He urged me to stop bargaining and quit giving away my old clothes and pens. He warned me not to return a gift for a gift, but only to make my thanks.

The idea sounded strange but it worked well. As a bonus, my attitude toward the Fijians changed. From this time on I was rarely short of food and found I got on much better with the islanders.

Dick Johnston, who had fallen out with his yacht skipper, sailed with me from one of the Fijian islands to the port of Suva. At the Suva yacht club Dick overheard someone mention the name of a girl he had once known in California. The girl was apparently on the other side of the main island, at Lautoka. Dick decided to take a bus and see if he could track her down.

So I was alone again on *Dove*, moored off the yacht club, when a club waiter came down to tell me that Joliette had been run over by a truck.

The waiter gave me the report as lightly as though he had been talking about the weather. He could not have understood that Joliette had been my shipmate for a year; that she wasn't just another cat around the harbor, now kicked into a gutter, but a proved comrade of the high seas.

At that moment I would have traded half my gear on *Dove* to have her back, to feel her nuzzling my ankles or to hear her crying for her dinner. I locked myself inside *Dove's* cabin and cried like a kid. I had not felt lonelier five hundred miles from land. There was no one to talk to, least of all some of those people at the yacht club who made no secret of their dislike of me—"that barefoot boy in torn pants."

At dusk and in savage gloom I went to the yacht club bar and bought a bottle of vodka. I returned to *Dove* and then proceeded to get totally and blindly drunk.

Two days later I was awakened by someone thumping the cabin roof, the noise hitting my eardrums like cannon fire. My mouth tasted of smoldering tennis shoes and the light streaming through the companionway looked like the inner fires of hell. I had the kind of hangover that could have been written up as a cautionary tale in the literature of Alcoholics Anonymous.

Dick was bumbling on about a girl—some girl who needed a place to sleep because her boss hadn't paid her wages and "she's rather short on funds."

I sat up and covered my eyes with my palms. "What are you talking about?" I croaked.

Dick took in the situation—the empty vodka bottle, the chaos in the cabin. "Look," he said, "it's just for the night. We'll fix her up somewhere else later. Come and meet her?"

"Can't you get out of here?" I said, and scanned the blurred face of my watch. "Wow! Is that the time?"

Unbelievably it was midafternoon. I hadn't eaten for forty-eight hours and was shivering with nausea. Dick came down the companionway and shuffled my arms into a sweaty shirt and my legs into oil-stained Levi's. Painfully I came up on deck and climbed to the wharf. I stumbled toward the lawn in front of the yacht club and raised my head.

This was my first sight of Patti Ratterree.

She looked gorgeous. Her head was thrown back in laughter, and she was wearing a brilliant blue island dress, very feminine. Her wheat-colored hair was long on her shoulders. I looked enviously at Dick.

"Nice," I drawled, and then to Dick, "I can see why you went to the other side of the island."

The girl stopped laughing, and with a slim, honey-colored leg kicked my bottom.

"What's that for?" I protested.

She studied me for a few seconds with mock gravity. "That's one of my friendly kicks, but it's just to remind you that I can look after myself."

Then she laughed again, her teeth marvelously white, her eyes very blue. There was a splash of amber in her left eye as if it had caught and held some of the sunlight. I grinned.

Dick was looking at each of us, at first anxiously and then with relief. He said, "You two are obviously going to hit it off."

The three of us returned to Dove and Patti picked up the empty vodka bottle. She didn't say anything. She just went over to the stove and started to brew some coffee.

Patti slept on Dove, but if anyone at the yacht club had played Peeping Tom he would have demanded his money back. I didn't even touch her hand. It wasn't because of inexperience. Kids grow up quickly in California, quicker still in the South Seas, and I was now in my eighteenth year.

But we were in unknown territory, strange and full of tension. It was not religion or anything that held us back, for both of us were as pagan as Congo pygmies, and I didn't care a damn what those people in the yacht club were thinking. Some dirty little minds were working overtime anyway.

Patti and I tried to pretend there was nothing between us, each of us putting up a front of flippancy, our conversation bantering, our laughter too easy. But it was like putting up a picket fence against the tide.

A few days later I asked her if she would sail with me to the Yasawas, a Fiji group beyond the usual tourist routes.

"We can get away from people there," I said quickly. "We can get into clear water. We can go diving together, go hunting for shells."

She was sitting on the cabin roof, her brown legs dangling over the companionway. She studied my face seriously for a long time. Then she nodded her head.

I began preparing Dove for the trip and was ready to start the outboard when I remembered it was Friday.

Lyle, Norma, Michael, and me on family trip to Tahiti, 1962, aboard our 36-foot ketch, *The Golden Hind. (Photographs are by Robin Lee Graham unless otherwise indicated)*

Leaving Ala Wai, Hawaii, on September 14, 1965, headed for Fanning Island, my first landfall, 1,050 miles due south in the Pacific.

Suzette and Joliette.

Two weeks out of Fanning, only 15 miles from Tutuila in the Samoan islands, a sudden squall hit *Dove*, breaking the mast. Using the boom for a mast, I set a jury rig and headed for Apia on the island of Upolo, where the mast was repaired.

The harbor of Pago Pago. I waited out the hurricane season in the Samoan islands from January to mid-May 1966.

In the Tonga islands.

Tongon dignitaries— time of mourning for Queen Salote.

Offerings for the late Queen.

The Tonga islands were called the "Friendly Islands" by Captain James Cook.

The forward cabin of *Dove*.

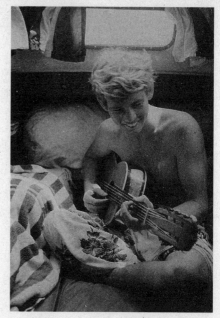

Fijian children
playing in the ocean.

In a lagoon off Savala. Patti and the nearly twenty-pound tuna she caught.

Fijian ceremonial dance.

Fijian father and son at bath time.

Navigating aboard *Dove*.

Repairing sails.

Sailing in the Solomons. The picture shows the wind vane my father and I designed. It was attached to a gear system and a trim rudder, acting as an automatic pilot to keep the boat on course. (*L. Graham*)

Dove at sea.

A feast of roast pig my father gave for the Savo islanders. The guests brought food too—papayas, melons, bananas, *bele*, kava, and coconuts.

Porpoises often swam along beside *Dove*; sometimes I thought they were trying to talk to me.

Sighting the sun with the sextant. (*L. Graham*)

Wreck of a World War II Japanese destroyer on Florida Island, near Guadalcanal. (*L. Graham*)

This was taken with a string attached to the shutter the morning after *Dove* was hit by a violent storm in the Indian Ocean in the middle of the night. The mast buckled and fell over the side; while I was hauling it aboard, I was thrown into the water and just barely managed to pull myself back into the boat.

Sailing under jerry-rig.

Mauritius, boat under jerry-rig.

A new mast was shipped out to Mauritius and I stepped it there with the help of friends.

Near Pretoria in the Transvaal. We traveled overland from Durban in South Africa to Johannesburg and Pretoria, and to the Kruger National Park. (*Patricia Graham*)

Robin and Patti, overlooking Gordons Bay, South Africa.

Navigating aboard Elsa in front
of a termite hill.

Kili relaxing.

Robin and Patti, South Africa.

Honeymoon trip,
South Africa.

Pete, harbor master's pet seal, Gordon Bay, South Africa.

Cape Town, Table Mountain in the background.

Around the Cape of Good Hope, which is *not* the southernmost point of Africa; Cape Agulhas, 125 miles to the southeast, holds that honor.

Kili and Fili playing aboard *Dove*, tied up on the river at Paramaribo, Surinam.

Paramaribo, open-air market.

Surinam River.

"We can't go today," I said.

"Why not?"

"I once made the mistake of sailing on a Friday."

She laughed. "You don't look like the superstitious type."

We did not sail till after midnight—two minutes after.

~~~ 4

Love and Blue Lagoons

THE NIGHT WAS MOONLESS. Suva's harbor entrance is almost five miles long, narrow, flanked by coral reefs sharp enough to rip the bottom off a freighter. Navigation by daylight calls for watchfulness. By night, and especially for the single-handed sailor, it demands full concentration.

The problem was to line up the pilot lights, which I knew had been well sighted. But still there was an eerie feeling because we could hear the noise of the surf on the reef. Patti sat beside me in the cockpit hugging her knees. She was silent and scared. I was pretty nervous too as *Dove* pitched and rolled in the swell. I put my arm around Patti and she rested her head on my shoulder. We kissed for the first time, very gently.

Then Patti went into the cabin to sleep. She was a bit seasick and rather miserable. The boat was self-steering well, but I stayed up on deck to keep a lookout.

We joked about it later, but we had taken a chance. When dawn came we struck calmer water on the lee of the little island of Savala. After the sun was well up Patti came on deck. She was still pale but managed to smile. She began to brush her hair and then to braid it.

She began to talk, just quietly. She spoke about her life, her childhood. She had been born, she told me, not twenty miles across the sprawl of Los Angeles from where I had been born. Her parents had been divorced when she was quite young. She had remained very fond of her parents, but the effect on her life of an unsettled though affluent home was to make her self-reliant. She had tried a short spell at college but found campus life too shallow and irrelevant. So she had sold her sports car, bought a backpack and hitchhiked with a girl friend through Mexico. There for the first time she met people with values as simple as their needs. She was convinced that the exciting frontiers were beyond Los Angeles, beyond America.

Sometimes she stopped talking and I could see her mind was far away. Then she would look up at me and smile and go on again. Rather shyly she talked about discovering in Mexico a strange sort of intuition that may have saved her life.

"I don't know how to explain it," she said, "but I have sometimes had a feeling of being able to see a little way ahead—as if time were a sort of path, and I could pick out my footprints before I made them."

I did not grin, and she continued more confidently. "I'm not a witch or anything, but I've sometimes seemed to know what to do, sort of where the thorns are. It was as if somebody was helping me.

"In Mexico my friend and I were waiting for a ride on a dusty, isolated road. It was as hot as hell and we hadn't seen a car for an hour or more. Then a truck came rattling down the road and my friend thumbed it. The truck stopped. The Mexican driver invited us to get aboard. My friend had already thrown her pack in the back when I grabbed her, and said, 'No, this isn't our car. Let's wait.'

"My friend was absolutely furious. We were madly hungry and thirsty. We stood there arguing on the road until the Mexican shrugged his shoulders and drove off. My friend sulked as we tramped on. Another car picked us up soon afterward. We'd gone on about four miles when we came across a group of people standing on the road. They were looking over a cliff. The Mexican's truck had gone over the side."

Patti paused and then added, "There have been other times like that. I must tell you about them sometime. It's rather odd and scary."

Her story had fascinated me so completely that I had not realized Dove was heading toward some rocks. I moved the tiller over and reset the wind vane. I asked, "Was it intuition that made you decide to come with me last night?"

Now she smiled, her teeth white as the surf. "That—and other reasons."

But I was to remember Patti's intuition in the months to come.

She continued to tell the story of her life, of how she had returned to Los Angeles with a wanderlust and had worked for a spell as a dentist's assistant to save enough money to travel again. With another friend she hitchhiked to Panama, staying at cheap hotels, finding little back-street cafés, always turning, as she put it, cents into dollars. In Panama she learned of an old but comfortable yacht going to Tahiti and was invited to join the crew, comprising a tough Swedish skipper, a German-Canadian cook, two Jamaicans and an older woman. The voyage took four months, with a six-week stopover at the Galápagos islands. It was not a happy voyage. The skipper was another Captain Bligh, she said, a bully who kept his own stock of food and treated everyone like dirt.

In Tahiti, Patti found, as I had as a boy of thirteen, that the Polynesians are people who have discovered their own source of happiness.

But Patti's goal was Australia. She had met a number of people who were enthusiastic about Australia offering a new way of life. From Tahiti she island-hopped across the Pacific to the Fijis, finding work where she could to supplement her savings. Her funds were low when she reached Suva and she was grateful to find a job as hostess on an inter-island tourist boat. Her duties were to point out the sights, to know something of the history of the islands and to hand out seasickness pills when water came over the prow. Returning to Lautoka after her first tour, the lecherous veteran skipper of the craft claimed that it was time for her to share his bunk. Without waiting for her wages, she jumped ship.

A few hours later, walking down a street alone, Patti heard a familiar voice shouting her name from a bus window.

"It was unbelievable! Dick Johnston! I'd known him in California," she said. "Does that bring me up to date?"

"And what does your intuition say about the days ahead?" I asked.

She laughed. "Bliss," she said.

And she was right.

We were children as we sailed the islands of the Yasawa group, kids reveling in sun and surf, knowing a glorious sense of freedom and timelessness. When the sun had risen high enough to warm our bodies and light the caverns and ledges in the coral reefs, we dived for shells and poured our treasure into *Dove's* cockpit. We found violet conchs, zigzag and spotted cowries, grinning tuns (*Malea ringens*), quaint delphinia snails, pagoda periwinkles, murex, tiny moon snails, fashioned with a jeweler's skill, delicate striped bonnets, tritons, augers and olives.

The cowries we loved best—some as large as a fist, skins silken smooth, dappled in warm browns. We swam together, Patti graceful as a dolphin.

Shell hunting among coral reefs is not all child's play. It has its dangers. Some shellfish are as dangerous as a rattlesnake. Under a rock shelf I found and fortunately recognized a cloth-of-gold (*Conus textile*). I pried it loose and, holding it with the tips of my fingers, swam to *Dove* and placed it on top of my drying Levi's. We watched its wicked-looking little proboscis come out of the mouth of the shell as the mollusk felt for its enemy. Then there was a faint swishing noise as the proboscis shot out its tiny harpoon into the cloth of my pants.

If the poison from the harpoon had pierced my finger I would probably have survived, but only because I was in good health. A few days earlier I had heard about a tourist who had picked up one of these rare shells. The harpoon had stabbed the palm of his hand and he had died in great pain three hours later.

While we were in the Yasawas I had a truly close shave. I turned over a rock on the reef at low tide and thought I had discovered a rare shell. But it was a stonefish, with a vicious sting in its dorsal spine. The sharpest pain I had ever known started at my finger and went up my arm.

The wound began to bleed a lot. There are plenty of stories of people dying from a stone fish sting, and I was really frightened. We were quite alone on the rocks. Patti tore the rubber band off her ponytail and made a tourniquet around my finger, which was already beginning to swell. The pain made me sick. Patti urged me to suck the wound and to spit out the blood and then she ran down the beach for help. She came upon a group of native women and with sign language and drawings on the sand she explained what had happened to me. One woman who could speak a little English told Patti that my finger should be boiled in gasoline.

I was not very happy when Patti returned with this prescription. We agreed that it would be better to take the odds on my surviving the poison than face the prospect of being blown up by boiling gasoline siphoned from the stove.

My finger throbbed for three days and it carried the scar for three months.

Apart from meeting up with stonefish and deadly mollusks, survival in the Yasawas gave us few problems. When we were hungry we dived for clams or fished for mahimahi. Sometimes a squid would jump aboard Dove. Squids are delicious. When there were no mosquitoes about we went ashore and built a fire to boil or barbecue our seafood. We drank from coconuts or we made drinks from papaya juice or fresh limes.

When Dove was anchored in a lagoon we did not usually have to wait long before being hailed from shore. Often there would be young girls standing there with baskets of fruit—papayas, bananas, breadfruit and limes. Sometimes we would barter for a chicken.

One scruffy-looking chicken so closely resembled a childhood pet I had called Henrietta that I could not bring myself to kill it. For several days Henrietta II was kept in a banana crate on the top of the cabin, and Patti fed it rice. When I decided that it was time for a chicken supper it was now Patti who pleaded clemency for Henrietta. But one evening, after a day of poor fishing, I concluded that Henrietta's hour had come. Patti was in the cabin, and on the excuse of sanding the deck I closed the hatches. To make sure Patti would not hear Henrietta's last squawks I began to sing. At least I made noises which were meant to be a song.

Patti's chicken fricassee Henrietta II was superb.

One learns from the sea how little one needs, not how much. These were our islands now, islands cut off from the world of concrete and steel, from freeways and television.

On the island of Naviti we climbed the shore and made our way through a grove of palms to a sort of meadow that overlooked the sea. Here we stood for a while soaking up the beauty of the morning.

Patti said impulsively, "Let's build a house."

We pulled down palm fronds and cut some poles. In a short time our house was built. It even had a front door that closed on leafed hinges. Whispering and secretive as children, we went inside and knelt together on the grass floor. The sun shone through the interweave of fronds as if they were tiny windows. The only sound came from the surf below the cliff.

A moment later and we were children no longer. It was a game no more. We had laughed and joked as we had gone about the building, just as kids laugh when they build a house in a back-yard tree. But now our playhouse was suddenly important, not like a tree house at all. If only, I thought, this place, this time could be forever—that here we could sleep and eat and love and sleep again.

In the cool light I reached out for Patti, felt the silk of her hair, the warmth of her body.

In the same moment there was a sudden pounding on the door.

Someone was beating our palm frond house with a stick, so violently that it threatened to crash about our heads. There followed a rough demand:

"Hey, you two in there, what are you doing?"

It was one of the islanders and apparently we had trespassed on his land. After freezing in alarm we roared with laughter and scrambled into the sunlight, stammering explanations and apologies.

I am no diarist and would rather face a squall than write a letter. To mark Dove's progress I always used the tape recorder. But with the best of intentions I had bought a typewriter in Pago Pago. Patti discovered the machine and began to put down brief impressions of these Yasawa days. Often while I was shell-diving I would hear her tapping away in Dove's cabin. Her sea-stained manuscript survived the voyage. It captures some of the color and the happiness of our time in the Yasawas. Here are some quotes from her diary:

AUGUST 25: Arrived at Waialailai after nice sail from Vomo. It's an island midway between the mainland and Yasawa group. Anchored around 2:30 and immediately got ready for diving. Swam with dinghy to sandy area and found quite a few nice shells. Went ashore and met the only family on the island. They seemed pleased to see visitors and presented us with papayas. Since it was still very warm at 4:00 we swam back to the boat over magnificent coral reefs, beautiful colored fish and giant underwater caves. Our best find was a beautiful triton, spiral-shaped and faultless. Robin has been looking for that shell for seven months. He spotted it encrusted in a coral growth about six feet down, decided to investigate and behold, it was the jewel! We'll have to polish it a little and peel off the coral. We also found large trochus and smaller edible shellfish. I boiled them all, including the triton, which did not taste as good as it looked. The spider conchs are the best eating—rather like crab. The island is covered with long yellow grass and reminds me of California—just a bit.

AUGUST 26: Swam with dinghy out to a sand spit which attaches Waia to Waialailai at low tide. Shell tracks abundant and we found many augers and olives. Dived about an hour and then swam back to boat. We always swim with the dinghy for safety's sake. It's not that we are chicken, just sensible—I hope. Spotted the yacht Apogee sailing for Yalobi. We knew it from Suva. It's from the east coast of America. Believe Al and Stella are aboard. They are collecting shells for the Smithsonian. Robin found enough eating shells for supper.

AUGUST 27: Girls came down to the beach and gave us some bananas. We mentioned we liked papayas. They promised to bring some next morning. We gave them a few ball point pens and kava roots. At 2:30 girls turned up again with ripe and semiripe papayas in a coconut frond basket. Lovely. Sailed over to the Apogee. Al and Stella gave us a wonderful supper.

AUGUST 28: I'm suffering from boils and so is Robin. Wonder what causes them? Big swell has come in and Dove is bobbing about. Robin decided to make spaghetti (ugh!). While rinsing the pot over the side he dropped half the spaghetti into the ocean and then spilled the other half over his pants. If I hadn't felt so sick I would have died laughing. Robin wasn't so amused. Boat moving so much in the swell we decided to sleep ashore. We gathered up blankets and medical box (it contains penicillin, pain killers, gauze and tape) and a can of applesauce. We were settling down to sleep on the shore when a boy came across and invited us to sleep in his bure. Rather horrified by rats running around.

AUGUST 30: Awoke early and found breakfast laid out for us by the family—neat blue homemade cloth mats and matching napkins, tea and banana fritter biscuits. The son of the family loaded us with garden-fresh vegetables to take back to Dove. Had a delicious fresh-water shower too. Powered Dove over to Nalawauki. Thought diving would be good but we had failed to notice the fresh-water stream that runs in here. Fresh water kills the coral and shell life.

AUGUST 31: Arose at 6:30 to a beautiful clear morning. We

sailed on a little and Robin wanted to dive but I wasn't too keen as the wind was chilly. The water felt wonderful though after the first shock. Terribly exciting diving on these coral reefs. Large caves are always popping up over unexpected ridges and sometimes big game fish come swimming lazily out. When the big fish see us they dart madly into holes. Any day now I expect to run into a shark. I suppose that would be the end of Robin Graham and Patricia Ratterree—but what a lovely place to die! Wind came up in the afternoon and we had a lovely sail to Naviti. When we passed a group of small islands we decided to anchor and dive. . . . Not too much luck but the spider conchs were good eating. I had a sudden feeling we'd catch a fish and then sure enough, just as we pulled out of Nanuyu Balava—bang! a big strike! With our combined efforts we brought in a beautiful barracuda, snapping and snarling at our feet. We'd both been dying for fresh meat and here it was. Pulled into small bay at 3:00, and immediately Robin wanted to go diving. I'd been in the water twice already and hated the idea of going in again. But rather than disappoint him I went over the side anyway. Returned to boat and made some chow. Cut fish into large steaks and made rice and gravy. Ate past the bursting point. Figured we'd have to do something about the remaining barracuda so we handed it over to two Fijians in a canoe. They gave us papaya. Read aloud to each other for a while from Tales of the Pacific. Then we went to sleep.

SEPTEMBER 1: Lazy morning. Woke when the sun was well up. Nibbled on the leftover fish and some awful rice pudding. Swam and dove a bit in a beautiful green patch. Found our first murex and one baby lobster—only a spoonful but great. Sailed for Tavewa. Magnificent lagoon. This is where the movie The Blue Lagoon was filmed. Poor anchorage on hard coral. Robin had to place anchors by hand in sandy patches. Made pea soup for lunch and fried the last of our bacon. Two natives paddled up in canoe and told us something of the history of the island. There are only twenty inhabitants. It seems that a Scotsman came here in the early part of the last century and married a Fijian girl. Most of the people are his descendants. They are rather inbred and odd.

SEPTEMBER 2: Fixed Spanish rice for breakfast. Natives came by in canoe and offered to fill our water bottles. I asked if there was a water hole where I could wash my clothes. Old man snatched my washing away and said his daughter would do it. The man sat down and told us story after story about the islands. He had it all memorized of how Captain Bligh had passed here when Bligh and a portion of the crew were set adrift after the Bounty mutiny. Apparently Bligh was chased away by cannibals. Robin wrote across his logbook, "This is Bligh Water." The island is divided into four sections and the main families feud like crazy. The old man's sister joined us. She is a riot—a sort of Mammy Yokum type with short braids. They took us to the store. You feel for the poverty of these people. There was so little in the store. Shelves were thinly scattered with cans of mackerel, one onion (which I bought for eight cents), matches, lollipops, gum, sugar, rice and one bag of tea (which I bought). They are so proud of their store, but it made me feel sad. One of the women took us to her bure and opened an old trunk. By the sound of the rusty hinges it had not been opened for years. It contained old family photographs. She pointed with pride to pictures of her two sons who had migrated to New Zealand. We felt suddenly wrapped up with the cares of people again.

One of the old men, named de Bruce, told us more tales of pirates and tribal wars. One story was about a chief and his twenty wives who were driven into a corner of the island where the cliffs are high. As they were about to be overrun by the invader he ordered his wives to throw themselves from the clifftop into the sea. There is still a feeling of death about the place.

SEPTEMBER 3: Old Charlie brought my washing back to the boat and our full water bottles. My washing is sparkling clean and fresh. Robin gave the old man his spare Coleman lamp. Wind came up strongly and we had some rather tricky sailing in poor visibility in an area completely honeycombed with reefs. Anchored at Nalova Bay, which has a shell market. The natives come in from the other islands and bring beautiful shells for the tourists who come here once a week on an island cruiser. The ship came in while we were there and we bought butter and ice cream off the ship—what luxury! We were invited to attend a dance, but I had one of those premonitions again, a sense of danger. I urged Robin not to go. We went anyway, and things did go wrong. First the dinghy came untied and drifted toward the reef. We went after it in Dove but we hit a reef. As Robin backed Dove off I retrieved the dinghy. When again looking for good anchorage, there was a jolt and crunching noise. Dove had hit again. If she had been a wooden boat I think she would have holed. But fiberglass is tough, and with help from local natives we got Dove afloat again. We were lucky!

SEPTEMBER 4: Lazy, lazy day. Robin sailed back to Nalova Bay while I just slept on the deck and soaked up the sun.

SEPTEMBER 5: Radio warned of strong winds on their way. We moved Dove to better anchorage shown to us by Fijians. The bay is so beautiful here, so blue, so calm, but we know the danger because along the shore there are coconut tree stumps—evidence of the ferocity of a recent hurricane. We waited for the predicted forty-knot wind, but it never came. Dove was as steady as a four-poster bed.

SEPTEMBER 6: We beached Dove at high tide and inspected her for damage. None, thank God. A Fijian boy on a rock nearby caught a fish and gave it to us. It was the only fish he caught—a gesture typical of island hospitality. . . .

There are gaps in Patti's diary, which was written to remind her of days that meant much to her. She knew as I knew that we had got too close to heaven too early, that our time in the islands must come to an end; that we would soon have to return to the real world again.

One day I noticed that she had stopped typing. She had put the typewriter back in the locker where she had found it. I asked her why, and she smiled and said, "I don't want to write the last chapter."

"Now who's being morbid?" I said.

She did not reply.

Patti did not record that we had sailed to the northernmost island in the archipelago, and the one from which the Yasawas take their name. It is a limestone island, quite different from the others, which are all volcanic. The cliffs of Yasawa island are full of caves, many with their own legends. We found a grotto which, they say, was once the refuge of young lovers. We dived under a submerged arch and swam for several yards under water before surfacing. At first it was very dark, and then as our eyes got used to the gloom we saw that it was bathed in a soft blue light coming from the water through which we had just swum. The air was supersaturated, chilled and quite weird.

Patti said, "I'm sure there are bodies floating here."

I was just as sure there were not, but the thought sent us scuttling back into the sunshine.

In one of the bays we had a quite alarming experience with a shark. I was setting the plow anchor by hand and Patti was on *Dove*. A shadow moved across the coral reef and when I looked up I was facing a long gray shark. It made a false pass at me. Sharks often do that before they strike. I guess it was figuring out whether I was worth a meal. Anyway, I didn't give him time to work out the answers. I broke the surface and jumped into the dinghy as I heard Patti shouting a warning.

"Wow, man, that was too close," I yelled to Patti.

"I'll say it was," said Patti. "It was awful. I could see him from up here. I just prayed you'd see him in time."

"Let's get out of here," I said as I climbed back aboard *Dove*.

We did. Actually this was the time when I turned *Dove* about. We meandered back through these marvelous islands to Lautoka. Neither of us spoke about the future, but both thought about it a lot.

A letter was waiting for me at Lautoka. It was from my father. He said he was flying out to join me in the New Hebrides. Some months earlier he had arranged for me to write my story for the *National Geographic* magazine. He wanted to take pictures of me for the story. I was to sail at once.

While I was readying *Dove* for the next leg of my journey, Patti found some Tongan friends to stay with, and she made plans to join a yacht sailing for New Zealand.

I intended to sail on to the New Hebrides at dawn on October 22. On the evening of the twenty-first a wave of depression hit me. It may have been due partly to the fact that I had spent the morning in a dentist's chair.

Dove was ready to sail at first light. I was sick at the thought of leaving. I could not believe that I could ever be as happy as I had been in the Yasawas.

Patti came over to say good-bye and then in the evening I rowed her ashore. She was wearing the blue island dress she had worn when I had first seen her at Suva. It was as if the past weeks had never happened, that our time in the islands had been a dream.

Now we stood on the shore, an awkwardness between us. Both of us put up a fence against the pain of parting. We spoke about the weather and silly things like "Don't forget to send me your address." Then she did a simple thing. She took the gold chain from her neck and put it around mine.

She kissed me and said, "It's only a loan. You can return it to me when we meet again."

Neither of us dared to think we would ever meet again. She stood there on the beach, quite alone, and in the fading light she watched me row back to *Dove*.

～～ 5

Battlefields and Love Letters

I WAS hardly out of Lautoka harbor, the sun not an hour above the horizon, when a strong southeast wind came out of nowhere. It whipped the sea into twenty-foot swells with whitecaps. *Dove* began to take a lot of water and was really shuddering. I was feeling seasick for the first time since leaving California.

Now I had a new shipmate. Two days before I left Lautoka Patti had come down to *Dove* with a little spitting kitten. It scratched my arm as soon as I had taken it from her. "We'll call it Avanga," she said. "That's the Tongan word for bewitched." I was to find out how well she had named him. Avanga was now bouncing around the cabin, and when I opened the companionway he looked at me with murder in his eyes.

It was easy to believe that the wind and the sea were trying to beat me back to the Fijis. I was pushing the boat too hard and began to hope that the mast would break so that I could have an excuse to turn the boat about and return to Lautoka or the reef. Just when I felt I couldn't take the weather any longer the wind dropped and shifted to the northeast. I put up twin genoas, and *Dove* logged 120 miles in the first twenty-four hours.

But the easier weather turned my thoughts inward and then to Patti. A desperate feeling of loneliness overcame me. I made some cinnamon toast, enough for two people, and pretended Patti was there to share it with me. I was going crazy with the pain of missing her, so I began to write her a letter. That helped. Patti had given me a small picture of herself, and I put it in front of me as I wrote:

> . . . It is real hard to put into words how much you mean to me, how much you are now part of my life. I was hoping when I left Lautoka for a real strong wind that would blow me up on the reef so that the trip would be finished. . . . I want to talk my father into changing the route of my voyage so that I can take in Darwin in Australia. Would there be a chance of your getting to Darwin so that we could be together again? Perhaps I could find a job there, in a uranium or gold mine or something, and we could live together —live in truth and happiness as we did in the Yasawas. . . . I've got up twin genoas now and *Dove* is going like fun, but the wind is taking me further from you. When I think of this I could die from the pain of being torn from you like this. . . . I manage to keep myself from crying out loud, but inwardly I cry—especially when I look at some of the things you left on the boat. . . . Only you will understand what it means not to have you here with me, not to have someone to laugh with, to talk to, to whisper to. . . .

The next day I continued the letter:

> Last night I went to bed at six o'clock, but I didn't sleep well. I'm reading a book about two young lovers, and the picture of you comes to my mind as I read, and I think how beautiful you are. . . . It's night again, the best time, because you somehow feel closer to me at night. As I write I feel I'm almost talking to you—almost. . . . I know it's hard to ask, but would it be possible for you to get to Honiara in Guadalcanal? I've simply got to see you again. I keep on taking out your picture and searching your face. I wish I didn't cry so much. I'm just a damn baby, but I miss you more than words can tell. . . .

My father was not in Vila when I arrived but turned up two days later with news of home and friends. It was more than a year since

I'd seen him and I realized how much I'd changed. I don't know that I'd changed so much physically, but I had in other ways. He spoke enthusiastically about Mike, Jim and Art, David and Steve, Judy and the other friends and relatives in California and Hawaii. They seemed somehow locked away in a closet in the back of my mind. I tried to remember their faces, their voices and the parties we'd gone to together. But it was like rediscovering a book I'd enjoyed as a child. The memories were nice but so distant— separated from the present by eight thousand miles of sea and a year of new experiences.

Between "now" and "then" the gulf was deep, and on the other side were bicycles, ice cream cones from the corner drugstore, ball games in the yard, a round of birthdays—all the interests of my boyhood years.

I was glad to hear my father's news, interested to learn that my brother Michael was now an officer and serving in Vietnam. It was especially good to hear about my mother.

With home news now reported, my father started to talk about his plans for my journey. He was enthusiastic about the *National Geographic* contract. His traveling bag was loaded with new film, his back with cameras. What was needed, he said, were more photographs of me talking to island natives, pictures of *Dove* sailing round headlands and up jungle creeks.

The subject on top of my mind never came up at all. I would have liked to speak to my father about Patti, but I was afraid he wouldn't understand. He was anxious for me to complete my global voyage and was worried about the slowness of my progress. I may have wronged my father. Perhaps if I'd talked to him honestly he would have thought back to his own youth and understood my loneliness. I'm sure we could have been close to each other had things been different at our first meeting in thirteen months. I should have understood his deep personal involvement in my voyage. I should have told him that if I failed then I alone would have to take the blame. I should have told him to trust me and to free me from his control.

But we kept our secrets. At least I kept mine. My father produced maps and charts from his suitcase. Each one was marked with lines and dates. With the Suez Canal now closed, we agreed to plot a different route, around the Cape of Good Hope. As we talked across coffee mugs in *Dove's* cabin and looked at the maps spread across the bunk I fingered the gold chain encircling my neck.

Hurricane season had come around again. I was not in a hurry to sail too far from land. My father studied prevailing weather charts and then announced that "risks are minimal." He boarded a freighter bound for Honiara in the Solomons. I sailed out ahead of him on November 8, expecting to rejoin him in ten days.

Navigation through the islands of Malekula and Ambrim was not too difficult, but staying awake was. I reported into my tape recorder: *I'm really nervous and scared because the winds are blowing in all directions. The winds seem to funnel down through the islands and the currents are strong and always changing. I've been without sleep now for thirty-six hours. I'm just so tired. I don't remember ever feeling so tired. I take a long time to write up the logbook. All the islands here seem to have two or three names. I've not had much to eat—too tensed, I guess. The volcano on Ambrim has a weird glow. I was going to stop off at Pentecost island to see the famous tree divers. They say that the men leap eighty feet from a treetop and stop their suicidal fall a few feet from the ground with vine ropes tied around their ankles. But the shore looked too dangerous for a landing.*

The radio warned of a hurricane buildup and I decided to sail on to Maewo island. Now I had to sleep, so I dropped anchor in the lee of the island and slept from three in the afternoon until five the next morning. I felt much better then and sailed on in lovely weather to Santa Maria.

I told the tape recorder: *Everything looks good. These islands are among the most beautiful I've seen. The sea is a marvelous blue and so is the sky. The islands are fantastically green with tropical plants and coconut trees. There is a terrific sense of peace here. Some islanders have just waved to me. Now I'm going to wash out my shirts and towels.*

Just as I raised Santa Maria, the wind dropped altogether. It was weird because the radio spoke about cyclonic conditions and the barometer began to drop.

As the sea remained millpond calm I powered *Dove* toward the Torres islands. The night of November 12 was the calmest I have known at sea, with water reflecting back the stars so clearly it was hard to tell where earth and heavens joined. I had a strange feeling of being adrift in space, stars above me, below me and all around. It was like being an astronaut without the cost of rockets or the problems of weightlessness.

Next day the radio reported the hurricane 120 miles to the east and shifting out of my area. The wind picked up so I sailed on more confidently for San Cristóbal. My father's freighter, I was to learn, had been caught by the hurricane's tail end. His ship had all but stood on her nose and the sturdy steel railings on the after-decks had buckled under pounding seas.

If that storm had caught *Dove*—as it would have done had I sailed three days earlier—November 18, 1966, might have been my last logbook entry.

The wind died completely again and I made only thirty-two miles a day between noon and noon. Captain Bligh had moved much faster under oars when he had sailed these waters in an open boat in 1789.

Avanga was no more pleased than I with *Dove's* progress, and without provocation he would arch his back, periscope his tail and fling himself at me from the cabin roof. I thought this was some sort of game until I saw the look of cold venom in his eyes and wiped the blood off my arms. The third time he attacked me I was close to proclaiming mutiny and putting him adrift.

I finally reached Honiara, Guadalcanal, on November 20, and broke my pencil with frustration when writing sarcastically: "Not bad at all—an average of forty-three miles a day since leaving the New Hebrides!" My father was not there but had left a note to say he was exploring the island of Malaita for picture possibilities.

At the post office there was a letter from Patti. It almost burned a hole in my pocket as I carried it unopened back to *Dove*. I wanted to read it quite alone. It was written on the day I had left Lautoka and read in part:

> . . . It has been the saddest day of my life and I find it almost impossible to think of living without you. How wonderfully close we've been. . . . I went through my things this morning to rearrange them, and I found that note you left for me and $20. Why in the world did you do that? You cannot afford to give money away. I immediately thought of sending it back to you, but then I thought, no, maybe I could put this money toward buying a ticket to wherever you go so that we can be together again one day. I promise I won't spend it until then. . . .
>
> I've just been given a Tongan remedy for boils. Perhaps it will help you. You take the white sticky sap from a breadfruit tree and apply it to gauze and then put it on the boil. The sap acts as a drying agent, they tell me. Let's hope you won't need this remedy and that your boils are better. . . .
>
> You'll be brave, Robin, and very careful, for I know one thing for sure. I know we are going to meet again. . . .

A few days later I received another letter from Patti. It was in reply to mine and she turned down my plea that she join me in Honiara.

"No, it's not yet the right time, Robin. We'll both know when it's time, and where we'll meet. . . ."

She told me how she had actually met my father at Lautoka. My father had stopped off there on his way to the New Hebrides.

> It was the strangest thing, but someone introduced me to a man who had just flown in from California. His name was Lyle Graham. Of course I knew at once who he was, but he didn't know who I was. We talked a while and he is so eager to see you. I'm sure glad he will be with you because he loves you so very much. It's killing him that he is not able to sail with you. . . .
>
> I hope your father didn't know who I was because I'm afraid we have created an awful scandal in the Fijis. The people here have branded me as an evil, corrupting girl. Oh my darling, I wish we

could tell the world about our love so that the world could understand. I hate the thought of spoiling your reputation. It doesn't matter about me. But if only they knew the truth. . . .

Last night I went to a Halloween party. My Tongan friends made me a lovely flowered skirt. But the party was just a bore because you weren't there. If only we could escape from the world and live together in peace and far away from people. Perhaps one day we'll buy a Tongan island.

Write to me care of the Royal Yacht Club in Auckland. I'll be finding work in New Zealand and saving every penny so that we can be together again when we both know the time has come. . . .

When my father turned up in Honiara he told me about the great battles fought on Guadalcanal in World War II. It was hard to believe because the islands were so beautiful, so much at peace. My imagination could not picture them raked by shells and bullets.

I teamed up with a young Australian my age. He had lived on Guadalcanal almost all his life and had collected his own museum of war relics—bits of machine guns, backpack radios, rotting boots, even bits of human bone. He had found many GI tags, some on rusted wire and in overgrown slit trenches, and he had mailed them to the Pentagon, from where, I presumed, they had been sent on to the next of kin of men who had died among the palms and in the jungle growth and along the shore.

The Australian showed me one place where the forest had been burned. He was still discovering live grenades. It was a bleak, sad place, full of death. I suddenly felt quite close to Michael in Vietnam—in some ways closer than I had ever been to him when he had roared his beach buggy across the sands of Morro Bay.

I tried to picture Mike hunched here in a jungle ditch, fighting in a war my generation barely comprehended. Perhaps it had been easier for the young men in World War II. Perhaps they had better understood what the war was all about.

We came across some natives wearing patched and bleached GI battle dress, and when I told them I was American the older men brought out souvenirs. One produced a gold watch, which had stopped. He said it was a gift from a GI whose life he had saved. He spoke so simply that I'm sure he told the truth.

These people, looking as they had looked a thousand years ago, had witnessed one of the bloodiest battles of history. They had seen modern weapons tear flesh and steel, heard the cries of men dying, watched aircraft fight it out overhead. In the quiet straits offshore, they had seen warships spit and thunder fire and death.

On the island of Florida, a morning's sail away, I almost stumbled over a water pipe leading down from an inland spring. The pipe had been built by U.S. Army engineers. Water still gushed from it, so I filled up Dove's small tanks from an aqueduct that had once filled the tanks of America's Pacific Fleet.

Solomon Islanders are shy, courteous and a bit nervous at being approached. But once you get through to them they are pleased to see visitors. One old man told me that they had never understood why the Yanks had fought for their land so fiercely and had then left them quite alone.

"Why didn't they stay?" the old man asked me. "The land is good—much fruit, much fish. The soldiers will be welcome if they come back."

On Florida island my father bought a pig from a local trader and then invited the islanders to roast it in traditional fashion. It was quite a party. Eighty people turned up, each bringing something along for the party. They brought pink papayas, *bele*, which is a sort of spinach, kava roots, coconuts, things like that.

First the pig was ceremonially strangled. It took quite a time to die and I felt real sorry for it. Then its hairs were burned off under fired coconut fronds. While it was spread-eagled on sticks, its flesh was tenderized with stones. Finally an underground oven was prepared with heated rocks and the pig was roasted for three hours. The preparation was a bloody business, but the pork had a marvelous flavor—and since we ate it off banana fronds there was no greasy wash-up afterward.

I managed to avoid drinking the kava here because it is traditionally brewed by women who first chew the root and spit it into an iron bowl. It is claimed that the saliva of the women—and only the most beautiful are chosen for the job—adds a special flavor to the drink. I took their word for this.

Savo island was only three hours sailing from Honiara, and I sailed there several times, mainly to study the weird megapod bird. The bird is short-tailed, black and brown, rather like a chicken, and it lays its eggs a foot or so below the sand. Each morning the islanders collect the goose-egg-size eggs from staked-off plots. If the eggs are left in the sand for forty days they hatch and the young birds are strong enough at hatching to take wing.

My father and I watched one fledgling struggle free, but just as it took flight a hovering hawk swooped and claimed its breakfast. I don't suppose the megapods can long survive the human and feathered predators. Although one of the islanders gave me half a basketful of megapod eggs, I don't know what they taste like because I lost them in the surf when my dinghy flipped.

The Savo islanders showed real interest when I swam from the beach to Dove, anchored two hundred yards off shore. I was puzzled until one of the older men explained that this was the spot where they threw their dead into the sea and where sharks ate them up. The reason why the islanders ran down to the beach to watch me swimming to and from Dove was that they expected to see me fight it out with one of the ten-foot morticians who patrol this stretch of coast.

In the previous six months thirteen villagers bathing on the water's edge had been seized by sharks. I heard one story—I don't know how true it was—that a hungry man-eater had followed an islander halfway up the beach.

A three-masted brigantine, The Californian, chartered by some scientists, was anchored at Honiara when I returned. The interest of the scientists was the weird behavior of a compass in some of these waters. The compass needle often swings all over the dial.

When The Californian sailed for the island of Malaita it gave me a tow. The yacht was crewed by three old friends, Chat Bannister, Larry Briggs and Mike Bennett. The scientists spent a fortnight in the area, and at night some of them drank so much that I wondered how they could carry out their experiments.

There are unusual ways of earning money in the islands. I discovered a very mixed crew of islanders aboard a half-sunk Japanese warship. They were diving to salvage nonferrous metal off the rusty wreck and sending it back to Japan, where the price paid kept a dozen Solomon families in style.

My father left for home a few days before Christmas. He was happy with the pictures he had taken of me feasting on roast pig and dancing with natives. I stayed on in the Solomons to wait out the hurricane season because the anchorages here are quite secure, especially in the salt water channel which cuts through the island of Florida.

No hurricanes came our way and when I felt the danger was over I sailed on to New Guinea. Now I was better off financially, for I had found a buyer who paid me forty dollars for *Dove's* inboard engine and I had rented out my spare genoa to another yacht sailing for New Guinea. The crisp Australian notes warmed my pocket.

I left Honiara on March 1, never anticipating that nine windless days later I would still be within sight of Guadalcanal. *Dove* just sat in the water. It was awful. Light airs just made me think of myself and my problems. On March 5 I celebrated my eighteenth birthday. It wasn't much of a birthday and I took no comfort from remembering that I now qualified for the draft. Before leaving Honiara I had written to my draft board, who answered that they "understood my situation." They told me to check in when I got home. I don't think they realized that it wouldn't be next week!

On my birthday I had some happy thoughts too. I remembered Patti running down a beach, lying in the shade of a palm, swimming like a dolphin in the surf. I remembered the scent and touch of her and saw her exploding in sudden laughter. I remembered the hurt look in her eyes when we said good-bye. But the distance between us was still increasing.

On the evening of my ninth day at sea a school of porpoises

came over for a gossip, and this, I noted in my log, *is always a good omen*. It was. *Dove's* sail, which had hung down like a shirt in a closet, suddenly filled, and my taffrail-log spinner recorded ninety-eight miles. This was better. But on the twelfth day at sea the wind swung the compass around to the bow and churned up twenty-foot swells. Once again I was beaten back on my course by the tail of a hurricane.

The fury of this storm kept me awake for nearly forty-eight hours at a stretch and my blurred memory of this period is of water pouring across the cockpit and through the cowl vent until everything inside the cabin was wringing wet. My precious Coleman lamp was torn from its moorings. It was like losing a family heirloom, because this was the lamp that had lit up *Dove* every sailing night since I had left Hawaii.

A fortnight at sea and the wind backed to the southeast—just the way I wanted it—and at last I was really on my way to Port Moresby in New Guinea. But man, I was tired! The fatigue had a strange effect on me. I'd have sudden spurts of energy and then a moment later it became an effort even to move a hand.

At no time did I have hallucinations of the kind that other lone sailors have spoken about. When Robert Manry went without sleep for forty-eight hours as he sailed his tiny *Tinkerbelle* across the Atlantic, he said that some strange people came aboard. I was especially interested in the hallucinations of tough old Joshua Slocum, whose story I was now reading.

Globe-circling Slocum was sailing off Spain when he fell ill after eating a meal of white cheese and plums. He went below and threw himself on the cabin floor in great pain and became delirious. He had no idea how long he had been lying there before becoming aware that his boat, *Spray*, was plunging in heavy seas. Looking through his companionway, he saw to his amazement a tall man at the helm. The stranger looked like a foreign sailor and was wearing a large red cap. Slocum thought *Spray* had been boarded by a pirate. According to Slocum's account, the sailor said that he intended no harm and "with the faintest smile" told Slocum he was a fool for mixing cheese and plums. With the seas still crashing about Spray's cabin, ailing Slocum went back to sleep. On awakening a second time and going up on deck, he found the stranger gone but Spray was still heading on a perfect course.

Frankly there were times aboard Dove when I wished a helmsman would come aboard. I wouldn't have cared less if he had been as ghostly as Slocum's navigator. But I truly did sail every westward ocean mile alone.

This leg of my voyage to Port Moresby seemed to last ten minutes short of forever. I was becalmed again and told my recorder: Dove made eighteen miles today by log but only ten miles by my chart, and since my taffrail-log spinner is mostly hanging straight down astern I have probably gone eighteen miles up and down.

My small shipboard library contained a copy of Samuel Taylor Coleridge's "The Ancient Mariner," and I knew exactly what the poem meant where it reads:

> Day after day, day after day,
> We stuck, nor breath nor motion;
> As idle as a painted ship
> Upon a painted ocean.

Even Dove began to croak and groan in protest, but these were sounds I welcomed in the silence of an endless sea. Without wind, the temperature began to soar and I recorded:

The sweat is dripping off my nose as I write up the logbook. I have to blow the drops away and I watch them splash against the bulkhead, where they slither to the deck like raindrops on a window. My shirt and pants are so soaked with sweat that I might just as well have had a bath. But what a miserable way to take a bath!

Unexpected happenings helped to keep me from going crazy. On March 19 I taped: Woke up and heard weird noises. I looked over the side and saw a turtle. I grabbed one of its hind feet, but it just kicked a little bit and knocked my hand away. This was a pretty strong guy. Then it returned. I guess it must have been feeding. I grabbed it in the middle with both hands and for about thirty seconds I held it out of the water. Then all of a sudden it pulled out of my hands.

That was too bad. I could have had turtle soup and steaks for a couple of weeks.

I was almost tempted to jump overboard and pull *Dove* with a painter. Then the wind at last came up again and *Dove* took a bone in her teeth.

On my twenty-second day at sea I wrote in my log that the journey from the Solomons to New Guinea had taken me longer than my voyage from San Pedro to Hawaii, which is twice as far.

Toward the end of this leg of my voyage I began talking to myself. I guess this would have interested the head shrinkers. I was mumbling away when a sudden increase in wind brought me to my senses. Looking about for the cause of the unexpected blow, I saw on the horizon a sight which just about froze me. It was a waterspout about three miles off the beam, black and snakelike. For perhaps half a minute I simply stared in a kind of daze. I can now understand how a snake is able to hypnotize its prey—why an animal is locked to the ground and fanged down when it might easily have scampered to safety.

I swung the tiller right across and told the tape recorder: *Boy, this is the ugliest thing I've ever seen at sea! It's really awful, and it's getting closer and bigger. I can now see the rainwater under the spout pounding into the sea. I don't know what's going to happen. I've just stored all the gear away below deck, but I guess if that thing hits me Dove will just disappear. The spout goes up into a huge dark cloud like an umbrella. Anyway, everything is battened down. It's a real ugly twister . . . but I think I'm gaining ground on it. . . . This is the closest I've been to disaster. . . . It's really scary, man. . . . Yes, I am gaining on it now. . . . What would have happened if it had been night?*

On the evening of March 24 I entered Port Moresby harbor in a heavy squall and with visibility so poor I nearly hit a wreck. But at ten o'clock that night I tied up to a mooring buoy, and with my last three gallons of fresh water I took a bath. Avanga was stinking too so I doused him with a bucket. His revenge was to chew up my only chart of Darwin's harbor. If I had caught him at it I would have made him walk the plank.

Next morning, after fixing up my papers with customs, I headed for the post office. Patti had known I was taking in Port Moresby and I hoped that letters not received in the Solomons might be waiting for me there. But everything was closed up tight. When I asked a policeman the reason he looked at me as if I was crazy.

"Good Friday," he said and, mounting his bicycle, added, "The post office will not open till Tuesday."

Fed up and tired, I returned to *Dove* and hit the sack. Perhaps I did wake up in between, but the next thing I remember hearing was the sound of bells on Easter morning.

By chance that Easter morning I met up with a charming Australian lady—I only wish I could remember her name—who had settled in Port Moresby years before. She took me to her home, where I wallowed in a hot tub. A humble hamburger, fresh bread and crisp lettuce were like a Thanksgiving dinner.

My hostess gave me the history of the port and told how an English adventurer exploring the Papuan coast in 1873 had found a break in the coral reef and named the harborage for his father.

The noon traffic jams and ice cream parlors helped me to understand New Guinea's huge leap from the stone age to the twentieth century.

In the Legislative Council there were men, speaking a lot better English than I did and wearing tailored suits, who, thirty years before, had decked themselves in feathers and pig grease. At the airport I saw tribesmen wearing *laplaps* coolly climb into aircraft bound for distant copra plantations.

I tried unsuccessfully to hitch a lift and fly to Mount Lamington, a volcano to the north that was famous for the 1951 eruption which killed three thousand people. One of the Port Moresby pilots said that "when you see a cloud over New Guinea you can be sure there's a mountain right inside it."

New Guinea is a fascinating frontier between ancient and modern man. Stepping out of modern diesel-engined buses and probably carrying crab folded in banana fronds are women tattooed from neck to thigh. This cosmetic surgery is still done with a thorn and mallet. In the "good old days," they explained, it was not a painful operation. But one day a young girl being tattooed laughed when she shouldn't have and the spell was broken. Now, they said, the surgery is just as painful as it looks.

On the Tuesday after Easter I was the first to arrive at the post office. There were letters from home, full of news and encouragement, a letter from the *National Geographic*, formal but friendly; and another letter which bore a New Zealand stamp. My heart missed about six beats.

Patti wrote of how she had arrived without incident in Christchurch and told excitedly that she had found the New Zealanders warm and hospitable—"really great people." She had found a job almost at once in a Christchurch hospital, but longed for work in the open air. Her second job was at an agricultural research station in Nelson, and this meant being outdoors all the time: "The sun is marvelous and I'm quite brown again."

I had written from the Solomons to tell Patti that my new route westward would be via the Cape of Good Hope and that I definitely planned to call in at Darwin in northern Australia. I had asked her if there was any chance of her joining me there.

Now Patti replied: "Darwin, yes Robin, I think I can get there. I've really been saving every cent and I have enough for the journey and some to spare. So I won't be a poor penniless wench when we meet again. After that who knows?"

Cables were exchanged between us, and by the time I sailed from Port Moresby on April 18 I had the best of all reasons for continuing westward.

In the Coral Sea I kept close to the land, remaining awake at night and taking catnaps by day. The moon was full and the twinkle of lights from the islands made navigation comparatively easy. When I needed a rest I would anchor off one of the many islands. At Dalrymple island I went ashore, taking Avanga with me in the hope that a spell on the beach would improve his temper. Avanga's beach behavior would have intrigued a zoologist. He performed like a dog, chasing lizards and hanging out his tongue, and I could have sworn he lifted his hind leg on discovering a tree. The unmanned light tower on the cliff was easy to scale, but when I reached the top I was alarmed by the view. *Dove*, far below, seemed to be high and dry. Actually she wasn't, but the water was so clear that it gave this illusion.

A weird thing happened to me on Dalrymple. At sea I had grown used to being alone, sometimes hating loneliness but learning to live with it. But when I was on land I had expected to see people, to hear voices, perhaps, or at least smell the smells of man —sweat, factories or even frying sausages—something to tell me that I was not the last man left on earth. On Dalrymple's island I was Robinson Crusoe without Friday's footprint in the sand. My feeling of being alone almost made me panic.

A day later, though, when passing Roberts island, I was given a clue that a nuclear war had not wiped out the human race. Someone tried to signal me with a mirror from a dark patch of coconut trees. I waved back and felt better.

An east–west current of six knots now began to give me the fastest traveling of my voyage, with *Dove* shifting over the bottom at about eight knots.

The night of April 28 was dark, and my new pressure lamp, a cheap one bought at Port Moresby, had broken down. At close to midnight I was in the cabin reading Ian Fleming's *Moonraker* when I heard a rumbling noise and a swish of water like a tidal bore. Next moment *Dove* was thrown over at an angle of ninety degrees, water pouring through the companionway. I scrambled to the cockpit to see a huge wave and, behind it, a black wall that seemed to be towering to the sky. *Dove* was being run down by a freighter.

If I had not been wearing my safety harness I think I would have jumped. All I could do was wait for the fiberglass hull to be crushed like an eggshell.

Miraculously the steamer's bow wave threw *Dove* clear and only the top of her mast scraped the freighter's flank. *Dove* rolled and bounced, and in seconds the long black shape slipped by and faded into the darkness. I stood there in the cockpit, quite stunned, water still sloshing around my feet, and then I screamed abuse into the darkness. The steamer had not carried any lights at all, and from her bridge there came no shout, no apology. I guess the man on watch must have been asleep.

My throat was as dry as the Mojave desert, my heart was thumping. I decided that from then until I reached Darwin and had bought another Coleman I would stay awake at night.

May 4 dawned beautifully as I entered Darwin's harbor and tied up at the yacht wharf. Officials were friendly but one demanded a hundred-dollar shipmaster bond for Avanga. I said I would give the cat away to anyone who wanted him. The official looked at Avanga, and Avanga stared right back. There were no takers.

My first business was at the post office, where I sent out two cables, north and south—the first to Hawaii for Mother's Day, the second to Patti saying, "Arrived! Where are you?"

~~ 6

The Hobo Makes It

THE FIRST FEW DAYS at Darwin were spent enjoying land legs and exploring this rugged frontier town. The surprise was the mixture of the population. Discovery of uranium at nearby Rum Jungle had attracted a lot of immigrants after World War II. At the local bars, cafés or in the fish and chips shops I would find myself talking to Poles, Czechs, Germans, Latvians, Hungarians, Greeks, Frenchmen and of course plenty of British settlers. The New Australians really seemed to fear the Chinese. A popular subject was the shortage of women. One of Darwin's suburbs is called Bachelor.

Several cruising yachts turned up in the harbor and there were old friends among the crews. One morning I was showing two attractive young girls over *Dove* (there are always girls ready to cook for a lone sailor) when I heard my name called from the wharf. I climbed through the companionway and squinted across the water and there she was—Patti, I mean.

Dove was moored quite a few hundred yards offshore. I rowed across and climbed the wharf. We just stood staring at each other. Patti looked terrific. She was so brown, so pretty. I couldn't believe she was really here with me. Then we flew into each other's arms. Of course I had to explain that the two girls who had come up out of Dove's cabin were ten-minute visitors. We had so much to talk about.

Patti had had quite an adventurous journey from New Zealand by plane, train and bus. A small aircraft had hopped her from Adelaide to Alice Springs in the heart of the Northern Territory, but still hundreds of miles south of Darwin. She was saving every hard-earned dollar, so typically she had slung her rucksack over a shoulder and had started walking north. It was just as well that this was the day when a bus ran on the isolated road. The sight of a young blonde in the wilderness is rarer than a billabong. The bus driver had rubbed his eyes, pulled up and invited Patti to jump aboard.

Patti then explained to the bus driver that she had been hoping for a car lift as she had already spent too much of her money on tickets. It seems that Australian Outback drivers have their own code of chivalry. He promised her that this leg of her journey would be free.

Covered with Australian dust and ten pounds under her best weight, she had reached Darwin's inner harbor two days ahead of schedule. Before hailing me on Dove she had found a wharfside ladies' room where she had bathed in the washbasin, set her hair and changed from her jeans into her only dress (very mini and feminine). She looked as if she had come right out of Saks Fifth Avenue by the time she shouted my name across the water.

We had a few terrific days together alone and we dreamed up schemes to buy a motorcycle and ride all the way down to Queensland. We actually bought one—from a con man, as it turned out. The machine was missing vital parts and never worked. You have to learn some things the hard way.

Then Charles Allmon flew in from Washington. He was a National Geographic picture editor and was loaded down with cameras. Charles was everything I wasn't. He was fortyish, crewcut, very tidy. He had been assigned to get pictures for my first feature for the magazine.

The trouble was, I think, that Charles had his own idea of whom he would find in Darwin—a schoolboy who had been president of his class and made the athletic team, a youth so full of daring that he had to be first cousin to the boy in the poem who had stood on the burning deck. Charles did his best to hide his disappointment on finding *Dove*'s skipper looking more like an Indonesian pirate and, after being so long at sea, not much more articulate than his cat.

I felt sorry for Charles but resisted his demand that I cut the hair off my ears and put on pressed shirts for his camera. He wanted better backgrounds for his pictures than the wharfs and main streets of Darwin.

"Arnhem Land," pronounced Charles over a dinner of inch-thick steaks. "Yes, that's what we need—pictures of you among the aborigines."

"How long will it take?" I asked suspiciously, calculating the time I would have to be away from Patti.

"Oh, just a few days," he said, focusing his eyes on the straggly ends of my sun-bleached hair.

Charles bought two air tickets and I was fascinated to circle over the north Australian coast along which I had sailed a few days earlier. In a few minutes the plane had traveled over as much ocean as *Dove* had managed in hours.

I turned to Charles. "I've decided to complete my voyage by air."

He didn't understand I was joking and for the rest of our air journey to an aborigine mission station I was given a sermon on perseverance, illustrated with stories of every adventurer from Columbus to Edmund Hillary.

"It's the next horizon that matters," said Charles. "Just think of it that way and you'll be home before you know it."

Charles was such a decent person, so full of optimism—of the kind of people who from their armchairs in Boston and Philadelphia had encouraged my forebears to open up the West.

He was a good photographer, passionate about lenses, light-meters and fields of vision. Actually I enjoyed our time in Arnhem

Land and learned something of the art of the aborigines, who are trying to keep their history alive with drawings worked on the bark of eucalyptus trees. After cutting down the bark they bury it in sand to dry. When the "canvas" is ready, they make fresh paint from crushed colored stones and the juices of plants. Their paintbrushes are made from women's hair.

Popular subjects for aboriginal art are their folk tales. One artist was illustrating the fable of the sun woman, who lights her torch each morning in the east and travels across the sky. At noon the heat from her cooking pot is so fierce that men are driven to the shade. The sun woman puts out her torch each day in the western sky, and at night she travels through a long underground tunnel until she is ready to light her torch again.

"Now why," I asked Charles, "should the astronomers have spoiled such a nice explanation of the day and night?"

Charles then gave me a long explanation of planetary mathematics. He was eager to see me properly educated.

When we returned to Darwin there was another problem for Charles. Patti didn't fit into his pictures—especially Patti aboard *Dove*. So each evening I would make a pretense of dropping Patti off at a harbor boardinghouse and then, after I'd said good night to Charles at his hotel, I would return and pick her up.

Patti was quite a cook. Each evening she would spread a folded *pareau* cloth across the orange crate table I'd fixed up in *Dove*'s cockpit. She would fix candles in bottles and then serve up a really good meal. A special favorite was steak and mushrooms with tossed salad and the local champagne. The people on the other yachts looked at us enviously. One night we invited Charles to join us. Patti offered him some local wine. Charles arched his eyebrows in disapproval. I could tell that in his mind we were like kids who had raided the cellar while our parents were at the local Rotary Club dinner.

The best spot near Darwin is a pool fed by a cascade of spring water. Patti, bikini-clad, found some ropes twisted around an overhanging branch. Playing Tarzan and Jane and making baboon noises, we swung out over the pool and dropped into the lovely clear water. It was a bit childlike but we were having a ball, while Charles snapped pictures from the bank.

The upshot of these days in Darwin was that a report got back to my father in California that my morals were shot to hell and that I had a girl in tow who was giving me booze and dope (I'd asked someone for Benzedrine to help me keep awake at sea). The report may have issued from one of the people on a visiting California yacht. There were several who looked down their noses at me.

Awful letters arrived from some of my relatives. I guess they had my welfare at heart, but what hurt most were the adjectives they used to describe Patti. They hadn't even seen her! She was the girl I loved! Even my inquiries about Benzedrine were interpreted as a warning that I was becoming a junkie. I couldn't believe that anyone, especially some of those closest to me, could make such accusations without hearing my side of the story.

One result of these accusations was that I resolved to try to become financially independent. An old cruising friend, Stewart ("Mac") McLaren, and I found a construction job at the Darwin power station. They were short of labor and no one asked me for my qualifications. I was told, though, that I had to wear shoes on the job. This was a bit of a problem as I didn't have any but I solved it when I found a pair exactly my size in a trash heap. I laced them up with copper wire and presented myself for work.

The work paid well and amounted basically to putting up steel girders. I was quite surprised to discover that without any training I could do more in a day than much of the local trained labor force. Mac was the foreman and I was described as "fitter's assistant." The job gave me confidence that I could at least earn my own way.

I was in funds again because before Charles flew back to Washington I'd been given an advance on royalties by National Geographic.

One evening when I returned to Dove I found my father aboard.

He met Patti for the second time and recognized the girl he had met casually in the Fijis.

I was sure my father would at once credit Patti with all the virtues. He took me aside and made it clear that his main worry was that Patti might make me abandon my plan to sail around the world. He told me that he was going to stay in Darwin until I sailed.

Contrary to my father's fears, Patti never held me back. I knew though how deeply she dreaded being blamed if I failed to continue the voyage. If my father had known it, Patti was really his ally. She gave me strength, and was always ready to let me go.

My father speeded up the provisioning of *Dove*, and he was standing there on the wharf when I boarded the boat, unfurled the new mainsail and heeled to the east wind. I'd been in Darwin just two months. Before leaving I shared my savings with Patti. This money, added to her own savings, would allow her to join me, if she would, in Mauritius—an ocean, eight weeks and about 4,300 miles away. It was just as well that I couldn't see the troubles ahead. Our next meeting did not work out the way we'd planned.

My last vivid picture of Darwin on July 6, 1967, was my father and Patti standing very close together on the wharf; my father short, wearing glasses, wiry, rather tight-jawed; and beside him Patti—slim, the wind catching at her skirt and hair.

We were bound together, the three of us, by bonds that none had the power to break. Both of them loved me, this I knew, but in such different ways: the one with a possessive love and believing he knew best just what was right for me and what was wrong; the other free and trusting. Patti was sure that there was order in the pattern of our lives—and that somewhere still beyond her vision we would find each other once again. I trusted Patti's faith.

My father and Patti were still on the wharf together when the morning mist and distance merged them with the light and shadows of the harbor. As I tried to recapture the memory of their faces and farewells, my love for them inexplicably merged too.

Then loneliness again. The old enemy had slithered aboard while my back was turned and my defenses down.

We are all made differently, of course. There are some of us whose peaks of happiness are higher and whose depression reaches deeper than the happiness and depression of others who cannot shout with joy or who never lose their cool. As for me, if I see grass greener than other people, if I hear sounds that they don't hear, then the price I pay is in periods of frustration and loneliness. As I left Darwin, *Dove* sailing wing and wing, my morale touched bottom.

Self-pity earns no credit, and I did not wallow in it too long because a gusty wind and whitecaps kept me busy with both sails and helm. My navigation had to be good if I was to find the tiny Cocos islands, 1,900 miles away.

Soon the color of the sea began to change from the pea green of the shallows to a deep blue. The thermometer dropped too. Two sweaters and a windbreaker failed to protect me from a rash of goose pimples.

Before I left the shallower water, the porpoises paid a call, grinning as they dived about the boat; and I had my own orchestra aboard—a family of crickets were cabin stowaways. Avanga pricked up his ears and tried to track them down.

Trade winds gave me good progress, and I averaged about one hundred miles a day. The job at Darwin had given me fresh initiative and I worked at projects such as making a pair of leather sandals, tying patterned rope belts and taking pictures. I fixed a camera fore or aft, tied a string to it and tripped the shutter from the other end of the boat. After Patti's cooking my meals were a bit of a bore, but I got a change of diet when flying fish and squid landed on the deck. Avanga always beat me to the catch, but there was usually enough for both of us.

I had hoped to make the Cocos isles in two weeks. It was eighteen days before they broke the horizon—almost seventy years to the hour after Joshua Slocum had raised their palm-fringed shores. As it had Slocum, the sight "thrilled me as an electric shock." *Spray*'s lone sailor had noted in his journal: "I was trembling under the strangest sensations . . . and to folks in a parlor on the shore this may seem weak indeed."

Six Australians were living on Direction Isle, one of the Cocos group, and they made up an air-sea rescue team, especially for the Qantas and South African Airways airliners which fly the long hop over the Indian Ocean. The Australians took me fishing and swapped my dead battery for a heavy-duty battery from their stores. They were nice guys.

I had wanted to visit the island inhabited by the great-great-grandchildren of John Clunies Ross, the Scots sea captain who had settled the atoll in 1827. In 1814 Captain Ross arrived at the Cocos with his wife, children, mother-in-law and eight sailors to take possession, but found that a man called Alexander Hare had settled there with forty Malay women. Ross and his sailors decided to oust the settlers. Putting up little resistance, Hare retreated with his women to the smallest of the group, still called Prison Island. The channel between the islands was narrow and the lusty sailors wore long boots. The women deserted Hare and the sailors greeted them enthusiastically.

Special permission was needed to visit the island, and as I had no permit I couldn't pay my respects to the 450 offspring of John Clunies Ross and his sailors. Although the islanders are inbred, today's community has found an idyllic life style. Civilized states might note that no one on the island remembers when the last crime was committed there, and that when a young couple are married they are given a house, a boat and a sewing machine by the community.

On August 1 I left the Cocos minus my one passenger. After eating up the crickets, Avanga seemed to consider me his next victim. The cat, I had decided, was really crazy. My legs and arms were covered with his scratches. It was time to split, and when one of the Australians offered to tame him I handed over Avanga without a whimper. I suspect Avanga attempted a coup d'etat among the island's feline community and I bet he got a dictator's deserts. I was sad, though, to hear a report on the day I sailed that the body of a cat fitting Avanga's description had been found floating in the surf.

Eighteen hours out of the Cocos islands I was hit by squalls. I was exposing too much canvas for the wind. At two-thirty in the morning I was sleeping in the quarter bunk when I was awakened by a weird rumbling noise. At first I thought I had hit a floating log or had scraped the top of an uncharted reef. Bounding topside, I found there was nothing on the deck at all. The mast had gone and Dove had been swept almost as clean as a rowboat.

Later I told my tape recorder: *The mast has been knocked down into the sea. It didn't break but bent over six feet off the deck and two feet below the old weld. Everything was in the water except the part of the mast which lay athwart the deck. I'd been wearing my lifeline harness while sleeping. When I came on deck I detached the harness because it was rigged to the boom, which was overboard. I struggled, getting myself all cut up, to clear the lines and get the mast and rigging back aboard and lashed down. Suddenly the boat lurched and for the first time in my life I fell overboard at sea—and without my lifeline.*

If Dove had been under way I would soon have been food for sharks, but within seconds—quite long enough—I was able to grab the rail and heave myself aboard. The water was fairly warm but rain and wind made me shiver. It took me two hours in the darkness to heave aboard the sodden sails and boom. I hacked free the twice-broken mast and let it sink to the bottom of the Indian Ocean.

I returned to the cabin and sat there shivering. Slowly I began to see that I was in real trouble. Up to then I hadn't been too worried because I'd been far too busy. Now my muscles ached and I couldn't go to sleep as I thought of the mess I was in. Dove just bobbed up and down on the choppy sea. It was then that I remembered how at Samoa I had forgotten the old sailor's superstition that a coin must be placed under a mast when stepping it. A wise sailor doesn't defy superstition.

Dawn seemed to take an awfully long time to come, but when it did I felt better. At least I had a cooler head and I began to think seriously what to do next.

Wind and current were behind me, so there was no hope of turning back to the Cocos isles. Mauritius lay 2,300 miles ahead—across an ocean in which many shipwrecked people had died of thirst and hunger. *Dove* carried provisions and fresh water for many months. My best chance, I decided, was a jury rig and the hope of good trade winds. Of course, if the winds failed I could drift in this ocean until they found my bones.

Fixing up the jury rig by stepping the boom with two shrouds, one backstay and one forestay, was a tough job. *Dove* now looked like a cork boat that kids sail on a duck pond. But the wind filled the shortened mainsail and I took heart as I saw white water at the bow. Wretched weather continued but the twenty-five-knot wind kept on my tail. To increase speed and to balance the boat, I sewed a small square sail from a bed sheet and attached it to the forestay. The wind soon tore this to shreds so I fixed up a second foresail with my yellow awning, patching a tear with a hand towel and a shirt.

Jury-rigged *Dove* would not now win a trophy for grace and glamour, but I was thrilled when my taffrail log recorded one hundred miles a day. Danger was ever present, and jibing was a problem. Several times big seas threw half a ton of water into the cockpit. Pumping the bilge kept my circulation going on chilly nights.

It wasn't all fun and games. On August 7 I taped: *A few minutes ago a huge wave broke over the side. I saw green water through the porthole for the second time at sea. My knees are still shaking. There's a lot of water in the cabin.*

Then the next day I recorded: *I was taking a noon sun sight when I heard a big bang. Another wave crashed aboard, soaking me and my sextant. This trip is getting to me. I felt like throwing the sextant right through the wind vane, but I thought I'd better not.*

After nineteen days at sea I knew I should be somewhere near the island of Rodriguez and was worried in case I might run into it at night. Fortunately there was a moon and I stood on the overturned dinghy strapped to the cabin roof and peered at the horizon. Then in the early morning I saw it and taped: *There she is, a long, solid piece of land about twenty miles away, I guess.*

I was tempted to pull into Rodriguez harbor, but the thought of Patti waiting for me in Mauritius kept me going westward. Five days later I told the tape recorder: *Wow! I'm right on course! I've waited so long to see Mauritius. Now I know my navigation isn't too bad. What a marvelous sight to see the island lift up out of the water, so green and round. It's taken me twenty-four days to get here—and that is the time I figured I'd take with a full rig.*

When I was tied up at Port Louis harbor a dozen deep-water vagabonds, including *Shireen* and *Mother of Pearl* from England, *Edward Bear* and *Bona Dea* from New Zealand, *Corsair II* from South Africa and *Ohra* from Australia, called in. *Dove* was tattered and battered—a proud little hobo among these sleek craft. But what a reunion party we had among old friends!

Patti wasn't there. From Melbourne she had tried in vain to find a boat bound for Mauritius. She had not had enough money for the air fare. Eventually she settled for an Italian ship returning disgruntled Australian immigrants to Europe via the Cape. Her letter said she would be waiting for me in Durban, South Africa.

That was a big disappointment, but there was enough work to keep me busy. *National Geographic* didn't want me to wait out the hurricane season and within two weeks they air-freighted a new aluminum mast in two parts.

Mauritius is the setting of Bernardin de Saint-Pierre's marvelous love story of Paul and Virginia, the children who grew up "knowing the hours of the day by the shadows of the trees, the seasons by the times which gave them flowers and fruits, and the years by the number of their harvests."

The story of Paul and Virginia reminded me of the time Patti and I had spent in the Yasawa islands, and I allowed myself to dream that one day we would again find the place and time "to learn the names of plants and birds and everything that had life in our valley . . . learn how to make everything necessary to the life of man, . . . and accomplish all these works with good temper which comes from health, open air and the absence of worry."

Sugar-rich Mauritius with its French atmosphere is utterly lovely with its blue lagoons and green hills. But it seemed to have lost the secret of the good life. While I was there the politicians were stumping on the eve of independence from Britain. Racial tension among the mixed population—whites, Indians, Creoles and Chinese—forewarned an uneasy future.

This time I was very careful to put a new coin under the mast at the stepping party on *Dove*. The coin was a Mauritian fifty-cent piece. So many guests clambered aboard that water began to flood my self-bailing cockpit. I chased off the guests while I plugged the scuppers, and then we resumed the party.

Waiting for the mast to arrive from America gave me the chance to backtrack with a new friend on an expedition to Rodriguez, a pearl of an island. Then on September 30 I sailed new-masted *Dove* to Réunion, eighty-five miles away.

Each of these Indian Ocean islands seemed to me to be lovelier than the last. I scented the flowers of Réunion as soon as I sighted its peaks, which rake the skyline. Perfume is one of the main exports of this tiny French possession. Geraniums, ilangilang and vetiver provide the special oils. They say that when Frenchmen go to Réunion to die they find life so wonderful they live to a great age. I'm not surprised!

On October 4, in company with the yachts *Bona Dea* and *Ohra*, I sailed southwest for Durban, 1,450 miles away. Knowing Patti would be there, I put out all my canvas. For three days the seas were calm, the airs were light. It was the calm before the storm. While I was asleep in the first light of October 8, the wind veered to the west and a different wave pattern on the hull awoke me. Just as well. My compass showed *Dove* had swung about and was going due east.

This was a day of a strange uneasy feeling. I could not pin down the cause. The new mast looked sturdy enough and I was making good progress, even against a three-knot current. But there was something wrong. Slowly my mind began to focus on Patti. I felt somehow that she was in trouble. I was not to discover the cause of my worry for many days—some of the longest of my life.

Extrasensory perception is not my bag. But perhaps when two people are very close they can transmit waves without material or scientific aid.

On the day of my anxiety (I was to discover later) Patti was with friends in Durban awaiting my arrival. When the morning paper arrived her host pointed to a newspaper story. The paragraph was short. It stated simply that the yacht *Dove* had foundered off the island of Réunion and that nothing was known of her one-man crew.

Patti's first shock was awful. But, as she told me later, she never believed the report. She had gone at once to the newspaper. The editorial staff were sympathetic and helpful and tried to check the accuracy of the story. Cables to Réunion didn't help. No one seemed to know anything.

Patti went back to her friends, who tactfully left her alone with her thoughts. In spite of the evidence Patti again put her faith in that strange intuition which had saved her life in Mexico. Her eyes told her I was dead. Her heart told her I still lived.

Her friends thought she was being brave. For nine days Patti lived through a hell of doubt but never lost her inner conviction that we would meet again.

I was now alone at sea, separated by winds, currents and darkness from the yachts that had left with me from Réunion.

The report of *Dove's* foundering came close to the truth. On the seventh day at sea I passed within seventy-five miles of Malagasy (Madagascar). I was reading a book, *The Ugly American*, when I noticed out on the horizon a weird black squall and as a precaution I reefed the main and genoa. At the southern point of Malagasy I had expected rougher weather from seas sweeping down through the Mozambique Channel. These seas have sent many ships to the bottom.

As a further precaution I put out warp, 150 feet of three-quarter-inch nylon looped in the water astern. The warp would help keep Dove's stern to the seas. The wind increased, and even under a jib reefed to the size of a dish towel Dove moved over the bottom at three knots.

Up to now in my voyage I had wrestled with the wind. Now I began to worry about the sea. I told the tape recorder: *Seas are towering thirty to forty feet but the warp is helping me to keep on course. Dove's not yawing very much. But there's too much water coming aboard. When I get to South Africa I'll have to board over the cockpit.*

That night the wind reached force nine. Huge swells kept on banging into the stern. I had experienced nothing like this before. The crests of the swells were curling into combers and often smashed into my back.

As Dove climbed up and slid down their boiling sides she began to shudder and groan as if the hull were made of timber. I reefed the jib to the size of a handkerchief—just enough canvas to keep her on course. There was no chance to sleep.

Next morning the storm was worse. Dove wallowed in mountainous seas. There was now a real danger of pitchpolling. I was unsafe on deck because a comber could throw me over the side and I was miserable below. But I went below and tried to read. That was when a huge sea crashed into Dove.

A little later I taped: *I really thought she was capsizing. Flying objects hit me. Everything loose was hurled about the cabin. When she righted herself I found everything forward had been thrown aft and everything aft had been thrown forward. Something solid dented my barometer case mounted near the cabin roof. The sea broke into a porthole and green water poured into the cabin.*

If another big sea had hit Dove at that moment I think she would have foundered. I had to get that porthole fixed in a hurry. It was quite a job. With the boat pitching and rolling I had to undo screws, wedge the plexiglass back into its frame and then screw it in again. I don't know how long the task took me—perhaps no more than ten minutes—but it seemed like an hour. All the time I was waiting for another big sea to smash into the boat.

The biggest swells, fifty feet or more, came at *Dove* in a series of three or seven and they were followed by lesser swells of twenty feet. The sea behaved like a boxer between rounds, panting and resting, gathering strength for the next attack. The surface would sort of suck and swirl and then lash out again, with hissing white-caps pouring water across the deck and cockpit.

In the fading light of the second day of the storm the swells appeared to be living things, bullying, cruel, determined for the kill. Above the noise of the storm I could hear water sloshing about in the bilge beneath my feet. The cabin was soaked, the deck a mess. The cockpit was filled with water and my water bottles, which I had stored there, were in danger of being washed away. The spray dodger was badly ripped and the companionway doors had been cracked with the force of the combers.

Dove seemed to weary as the storm progressed. She groaned and protested all the time. Every now and then I would stand up and grab the boom to search the horizon for some clearing of the weather.

In a sea like this the real danger was not so much that the boat would be swamped, unless the portholes were forced again. Ocean-going yachts are built for heavy seas. They are buoyant enough to take several tons of water aboard. *Dove* was deep-keeled for her size and with everything battened down she could ride these waves as long as I had strength to keep her stern toward them. The real danger was that after sliding down a sea her bow would plow into the bottom of the trough. The boat would then pitchpoll, and corkscrew under the water.

Although it is a terrifying experience, yachts can often survive a corkscrew. The yacht *Ohra*, which had left Réunion with me, managed to do so, and probably in an extension of this same storm now battering *Dove*.

It is hard to remember what thoughts I had at the height of the storm. Some fear, yes, fear touching the edge of panic. But the instinct of survival is what takes over in the end. My survival depended on my keeping Dove's stern to the sea and on keeping awake.

I'd been awake for almost forty-eight hours, and now thunder and lightning increased the tension and the noise of the storm. It was fantastic. Brilliant flashes lit up the monster swells and filled the cabin with green light. Then the thunder roared above the noise of the sea. For the first time in my voyage I felt that Dove would not make another port. The seas were too big for her after all and I too tired to help her.

My battery-powered tape recorder was soaked and the reels wouldn't turn. So I turned the reels by hand to make one last recording. I said: *I've just prayed to God, and I prayed long and hard to make the sea and wind calmer. I prayed, "God or whoever you are, please help me."*

I remember thinking at this time of a story I'd heard in my childhood of Jesus calming a rough sea. I prayed with my arms locked round the tiller.

That was the moment when the storm began to abate. The huge swells stopped coming at me. I went to sleep. When the sun woke me up next morning, October 14, the wind was down to fifteen knots. The sea was sparkling and gentle.

I unfurled the main and genoa, took an LOP and reset my course for Durban.

~~~ 7

Drumbeats and Bridal Suite

WHAT TO EXPECT OF AFRICA? Hollywood had fixed images in my mind of tangled jungles and lions under the bed, of natives dancing around big iron pots, of rivers swarming with crocodiles and outpost mission stations manned by men in pith helmets.

The first surprise was on October 21 when I reached Durban. I hadn't expected a skyline like San Francisco's. And anyone who has not been to Africa cannot understand that Africa has its own blood beat, a sort of rhythm that you can't hear but feel.

Beyond the modern high-rise cities where the paved roads lead to red dirt tracks and the huge vistas of the veld, the throb seems to come from deep inside the earth. In Africa you get the feeling that you are seeing the planet earth before man began to ravage nature.

I was to spend nine months in South Africa and I was tempted to stay there until the sun bleached my bones. It was a fantastic time.

I turned into Durban's broad harbor and as I approached the

basin of the Royal Natal Yacht Club a figure on the mole waved and shouted at me. I didn't take any special notice until I heard my name. It was Mac McLaren, who had worked with me at the Darwin power station. Mac dived into the water and swam to Dove. When I had pulled him aboard he told me that he had been keeping a watch for Dove along with Patti. Between gulps of air he explained how soon after Patti had arrived she had read the newspaper story of Dove's foundering. Patti, he said, was waiting for me on one of the ocean cruisers in the yacht basin.

After I cleared customs, Mac took me to the yacht where Patti was and there, in the cabin, I held her in my arms again.

Neither of us had ever spoken of marriage Life had seemed too uncertain to be tied by legal bonds. Both of us were cautious of marriage, anyway, for there were too many of our relatives and too many of our parents' friends whose marriages had broken down. We knew married couples as compatible as a mongoose and a cobra. Then too, by the calendar if not by experience, we were very young.

For both of us it was marvelous just to be together when we could. This was all we had asked for. A wedding and a starchy reception at a country club, a honeymoon car covered with confetti and rattling with tin cans could not pull us closer together than we were.

But at our Durban reunion a new idea crossed my mind. I longed to give Patti a pledge that she meant much more to me than just being a sailor's wife. I wanted to show her that I believed the day would come when we would not be torn apart by a fair wind and the need to make another port.

We had only ten minutes together in the cabin before someone tapped on the door of the companionway. A staff writer of National Geographic came in and introduced himself. For the next week the writer and I were cooped up together as we worked on the manuscript and captions of my first feature for the magazine.

Patti had found a room in a small hotel two blocks behind the plush ones on the seafront. From there we discovered a side-street café with a fantastic atmosphere where a good meal with wine cost only a couple of dollars. Why pay for orchestras and waiters not worth their tips?

On the day the magazine staffman returned to America, Patti and I strolled down one of Durban's broad boulevards. As we passed a jeweler's shop window a gold ring with a strange Oriental design caught my eye. I tugged at Patti's arm.

Her face was quite a study as I asked the jeweler to put the ring on the third finger of her left hand. It was a perfect fit.

"There," I said. "As soon as I saw it I knew it was made for you."

She held out her hand and looked at it a moment, then said, "It's fantastic, Robin, but what's it for?"

"We're engaged, of course! When do we get married?"

She dropped her hand to her side and looked at me. "Now, Robin, don't let's be hasty." She was laughing.

But I was serious. The jeweler shifted from one foot to the other.

"I just want you," she said gravely, "and of course this absolutely lovely ring."

When we returned to the hotel the proprietress at once spotted the band on Patti's finger. "Oh, what a pretty ring, Mrs. Graham," she said breezily. "I was telling my husband you must have lost it."

"I didn't own a ring until half an hour ago," said Patti with the blandest smile.

The proprietress sniffed, and not knowing where the conversation would take her, retreated behind her desk. But even in the guttural English of the Afrikaner I liked the sound of Patti being called Mrs. Graham. That night when we were in each other's arms I whispered, "Now, Mrs. Graham, when shall we make it legal?"

She tilted her head and kissed my chin. "I've always wondered if your intentions were strictly honorable."

"Very honorable," I said, "and I'm quite serious."

"Are you? Or is it that you don't like what the hotel proprietress is thinking and the looks they give me down at the yacht club?"

"Forget them," I said. "They're jealous of the guy with a beautiful girl in a red bikini."

Patti was silent a moment, then asked, "How does the song go? Will you still love me when I'm sixty-four?"

"And when you're a hundred and four if you stay as trim as you are."

"And if I don't?"

"I'll chase you around the island before breakfast."

Again she was silent and then she whispered, "How big's the island?"

"That sounds like an acceptance of my proposal," I replied.

She didn't laugh this time. She said, "You know it doesn't have to be marriage, Robin. I wouldn't want you ever to feel that you can't leave me. I don't want you ever to think that you owe me anything. I love you. That's why I'm here. We're happy. We're young. Life is a long time. I hope it's a long time and that as much as possible will be with you. Please don't think that by giving me a piece of paper you'll change what I feel for you. I can't love you any more than I do now. I don't think I can."

Next morning we went to the Durban magistrate's court to get married. The official immediately asked my age. When I told him I was eighteen he said we would need the notarized consent of parents or guardian, as I was still a minor. This was a shock. I couldn't understand why anyone should still be able to control me when I was half a world away from home. Patti returned to the yacht club and I went to the post office, where I wrote my parents an air letter and explained I needed their consent to marry Patti.

It was a lovely day and as I walked back to the yacht club I couldn't think of any reason for waiting for my parents' reply and all the legal stuff. I found Patti at the club and led her outside by the hand.

"Where're we going?" she asked.

"You'll find out," I said.

She continued to look puzzled but didn't ask any more questions as I walked her along the beach. We found an empty spot in the sand and sat down in the sun.

I said, "I've been doing a bit of thinking and I don't see why we should wait for anyone's consent to get married. We love each other. That's enough. Besides, I hate what people are thinking about you."

"Do we have to worry what other people think?" said Patti.

"Yes, we do," I replied, "because it makes me mad."

I took the ring off her finger and as I put it on again I said, "Patti, I don't know the words of the marriage ceremony. I just know that I want to spend the rest of my life with you. There now; from this day we are man and wife."

It was as simple as that.

Actually, when my parents later replied to my letter they refused me permission to marry. They talked about my completing the voyage and that there'd be time enough—that sort of thing. They believed they knew best what was right for me. I wrote back and told them Patti and I considered ourselves married anyway.

When we walked back along the sand of Durban's beach we felt marvelously happy. It was all so neat. We both knew our marriage would last as long as we lived. I said, "Okay, where do we go for our honeymoon?"

That evening at the yacht club we had a sort of wedding party. Everyone else thought it was an engagement party, but that didn't matter. Mac was there and some other people off the yachts, and it was fun. The next day we bought a well-used Japanese motorcycle, two saddlebags and a blue pup tent and then we set off at once to explore Africa—or at least the southern part of it.

We traveled up the coast to Saint Lucia and turned north to Umfolosi Game Reserve in Zululand, the home of the rare white rhinoceros. At the ranger's office inside the reserve we asked for a local map. The ranger was helpful and told us where the rhino were feeding.

"But keep inside your car," he warned. "Those rhinos can move when they think they're threatened."

"Don't worry," I said. "We've got a fairly reliable motorcycle."

The ranger stopped in his tracks. "Motorcycle? You're not allowed in the reserve on a motorcycle. How did you get through the gates? No, never mind, just get out of the park as fast as you can—and good luck."

Since we had traveled half across the world, we decided that before leaving the park we'd do some exploring on our own. Patti had christened the motorcycle Elsa. She named it for the lioness in the film *Born Free*. With the two of us aboard, Elsa had difficulty making hills steeper than one-in-eight gradient. The trick, we learned, was to approach a hill at full throttle and if it wasn't too long we usually made the top in the style of the little red engine.

Ahead of us was a hill steep enough to test Elsa's one small cylinder, but there was a chance to make the crest if I could persuade the machine to touch 45 mph on the downward gradient. Yelling to Patti over my shoulder to hold on to my belt, I turned over the hand-grip throttle as far as it would go. Elsa kicked up a cloud of red dust as we roared into the shallow valley. Just as we began the ascent a huge mud-gray shape as solid as a locomotive ambled out of the tall grass and right across our path.

I had had my share of hazards at sea, but the prospect of hitting a white rhino broadside at three-quarters of a mile a minute looked as if it would top every story in my book.

Patti told me later she had simply closed her eyes. I will swear that Elsa's starboard handlebar cut a permanent groove in the armored butt of the enormous beast.

We traveled another mile or two in awed silence and then I turned Elsa off the dirt road onto a grass track. We pitched our pup tent under a tree and after a dinner of fried *boerewors* (South African spiced sausage) we listened to the night sounds of wildebeests and leopards.

Then we slept—but not for long. Patti nudged me awake and I knew at once why she was as coiled as a watch spring. Just outside our tent something very large was tearing up the shrubbery. Pretending courage I didn't possess, I lifted the flap and shone my flashlight around. About ten yards away the light was reflected back from a single, unblinking red eye.

I am sure there are strategies used by unarmed big game hunters when they see one red eye raised five feet off the ground and within a wino's spitting distance. But as I had not read up on the travel books, I fell back on the suburban drill when the neighbor's German shepherd approaches with bared fangs.

"Shooo!" I hissed into the night.

Nothing happened. Without much comfort I remembered that the eyes of a rhino are so placed that when it stands sideways only one eye can be seen. As Einstein said, some seconds last longer than others. At this moment the seconds were beating out at about fifteen to the minute. Then, with a rumble that we felt through our sleeping bag, the owner of the red eye took off into the night.

At breakfast we were heavy-lidded, but felt some kinship with all those pioneers who have braved the perils of the Dark Continent.

We traveled north, skirting Swaziland—the Switzerland of Africa —and meandered through the lush low veld, discovering mountains of fantastic beauty, little African villages of thatched rondawels and places with romantic names—Bushbuck Ridge, Pilgrim's Rest, Acornhoek, God's Window, Phalaborwa, Tzaneen. When the sun set we pitched our tent, cooked a meal over an open fire and listened to the sounds of Africa—the howl of jackals, sometimes the beat of drums and, when on the edge of the two-hundred-mile fence of the famed Kruger National Park, the unforgettable roar of lion.

For a few days we took aboard an interesting traveling companion—a chameleon about fourteen inches long. We christened him Clyde, and for many miles he sat perched on Elsa's handlebars looking out at the countryside through prehistoric eyes. Clyde never recovered his composure after our only mishap. Elsa skidded on a patch of oil and Patti and I were thrown into a ditch with little more damage than a grazed knee and bruised elbow. When we had brushed ourselves down we found Clyde tiptoeing into the bush. Only his dignity had been hurt so we repositioned him on his perch. But from then on Clyde kept one eye anxiously on the road ahead and the other fixed accusingly on my face. Clyde's leap from the mists of time to the age of the motorcycle was obviously too rapid for his pleasure.

Marvelously content with our own company, we avoided big towns and rarely met up with people, black or white. But whoever we met we found friendly and hospitable. It seemed strange to us and sad that in a country condemned for its racial policies the individuals—the African, Afrikaner and English-speaking settler—should share in common a rare and charming hospitality. Several Afrikaner storekeepers and farmers loaded us with fruit and vegetables and refused to take payment. Africans along the roads greeted us with waves and pearly smiles.

Sometimes we would leave Elsa at the roadside and trek barefooted into the veld to explore grottoes, vast plains, forest trails, all hauntingly beautiful. We would bathe under mountain cascades and stretch out in the sun, and occasionally be chased by a colony of baboons. At dawn we would stalk herds of grazing impala, the most graceful of the antelope. Then, alerted by our scent or the snapping of a twig, the whole herd would bound for the cover of the trees—a flash of sunlit fawn and white against the gray of mountain rocks or the lush green of the new grass and wild mimosa.

We possessed no calendar, not even a watch between us. Time was measured by the angle of the sun and by nights filled with the perfume of exotic flowers, and always the inexplicable throb beating out the rhythm and the harmony of nature.

At one campsite near Acornhoek we so loved the peace and beauty of the land, its warmth and color and great views, that we made inquiries about buying a stretch of the African veld. What, we asked ourselves, compelled us on? Here we could build a rondawel like the ones the Africans build, and plow soil eager to yield all the food we needed. Here we could cut ourselves off from the conformity and drudgery, the smog, smells and overcrowding of the society into which we had been born.

But even as we weighed our arguments and measured out ten acres bordered by a creek, we knew that it was not yet the moment for our retreat. So we packed our saddlebags again, mounted Elsa and headed toward the coast.

Back at Durban I gave Dove a close inspection and realized she was in worse shape than I had at first believed. The Malagasy storm had more than bruised her. Water had seeped into the points where the deck joined the hull. The wood sandwiched between the fiberglass panels had begun to rot. In her present state Dove would not again survive high seas or gale.

For two months I worked on repairing the boat, and before sealing the decks to the hull I lifted out the cockpit and decked her over aft. The cockpit had served me little purpose and was generally filled with gear better stored below. In a heavy sea the cockpit had proved a danger. It was capable of scooping up half a ton of water.

The job of fitting and fiberglassing was hard work and frustrating too, but I had a helpmate now in Patti, who fetched and carried timber, screws and resin and who cooled my temper with cold beer and soft answers.

On March 8, Dove was ready for the sea again. Patti saw me leave the yacht basin and then she set off on Elsa for East London, 250 miles down the coast. If the wind was fair we would be together again in three days. But I'd traveled barely twenty miles before the wind quit altogether and I told my tape recorder:

Good old weather reports! They promised a northeaster, but where is it? There's a big hotel on the shore a couple of miles away and I've been looking at its windows for an hour.

The day of leaving port is always the longest part of a journey. Landmarks along the coast ridicule a small sailboat's progress. On the first day out you think about the miles ahead and the loneliness.

Toward noon the wind picked up, not from the northeast as promised on the radio but from the southwest. It was coming from the direction I wanted to go.

I taped: *I never want to beat. If the wind is forward of the* beam and fifteen knots or more, I say forget it. No use fighting this weather. I turned Dove about and headed back to Durban, making the twenty-five-mile return trip in a very fast three hours.

Of course Patti was gone. The sun-washed, sparkling Durban that had welcomed me in October was now drab, cold, unfriendly. It was like returning to a house that had once been a well-loved home, but finding it empty, shuttered, smelling of mice and mildew. How weird, I thought, that one small girl could change the character and climate of a city.

Late that afternoon I walked the beach and found the spot on the sand where we had had our "wedding." The sand that had been warm and silken on that day was gray now, chilly to the touch.

In the night the wind freshened to a gale, howling through the harbor and thrashing rigging against Dove's mast—a miserable noise that lasted thirty-six hours. When I sailed again I had little better luck. The sea lanes were crowded with shipping forced around the Cape by the closure of the Suez Canal and I was obliged to stay awake at night to avoid collision. It was pretty hairy sailing. I hate taking pills, even aspirin, but I knew that to sleep for ten minutes could spell disaster, so I swallowed two Benzedrines and peered into the darkness, shifting the tiller whenever I saw or imagined a gray shape ahead.

The wind rose to thirty knots and again came right out of the southwest. Scudding heavy clouds were a few hundred feet above the mast. On my second day at sea I reefed the sails and slept for perhaps three hours. When I awoke the land was out of sight. A current had taken me far out. I told the tape: Now I'm completely lost. I should be somewhere off the Wild Coast . . . but for all I know I might be off the South Pole.

At Durban they had told me weird tales of ships vanishing without trace on this stretch of ocean between Durban and East London. The best-known story was the one about the Waratah, sailing for Australia in the last century with a large number of women aboard. She just vanished. One theory was that the ship had been wrecked on the Wild Coast, where the men had been murdered and the women seized—accounting for the light skins of the Pondo Africans in this area.

On the fifth day out, without hope of finding my position from sun or stars, I was lucky to pick up a strong land beacon on my radio. By turning my radio to the strongest point of the signal I homed in on the coast and sailed past East London's harbor wall on March 14.

No sign of Patti. Her route would have taken her through the Transkei, the biggest of the native territories. With racial tension high, a white girl alone on a motorcycle could well have been attacked. I trudged to a police station, where a heavy-jowled sergeant at the desk grunted negatives to my inquiries about road accidents. Miserably I returned to *Dove*.

That night I had a horrible and vivid dream. I saw Patti crumpled up in a ditch, beside her the twisted frame of Elsa. So clear was the dream that I saw her blood-wettened hair across her face, her fingers stiff and curled, the ring clearly on her finger. I awakened shivering, cursing the sense of duty which had compelled me to sail on alone.

Of course it was only a dream. When the sun was up I walked down the seafront esplanade and we saw each other when five hundred yards were still between us. Both of us began to run. The shipping people had told her that the storm would delay me two more days.

It took ten days before I could summon courage to sail again. It wasn't that I feared the sea but the moment of our parting. I told Patti, "If I were stronger I wouldn't need you the way I do."

She never tried to hold me back. She never clung to my body or my spirit. She was there when I needed her, but ready to free me the moment I was ready to sail on. This time, though, before riding out of town Patti waited on the harbor wall to be sure that *Dove* was heading westward along the coast. *Dove* had barely hit the swells outside East London's harbor when the wind veered to the southwest. I turned back into port once again and Patti helped me tie up *Dove* for another night. Next day the northeaster held and *Dove* took only thirty-six hours for the short leg to Port Elizabeth.

Simply knowing that Patti would be ahead of me and waiting at quayside, wharf or on the cliffs along the coast kept me sailing through some of the most discouraging weather I had struck. Home now was where Patti was, and Patti was always a port ahead.

Twice I tried to leave Port Elizabeth and twice I failed as the wind swung the compass around to my bow. The third time out, I still had to beat against a southwest wind. I began to think this was an omen, a sort of warning to stop my global voyage. Suddenly the idea struck me that one sure way to end the voyage was to wreck the boat deliberately.

It would be simple enough to blow up the life raft, scuttle *Dove* and then paddle to the shore. My mind had already half written the letters I would send home—the story of how *Dove* must have hit some rock or hidden wreck and foundered, and how happily I had been close enough to shore to save my life. Never again would I have to face the cruel gray sea alone.

In a frenzy of energy I collected my passport, documents, logbook and money and packed them into the raft.

In now confessing this planned deception I would like to be able to claim that a sense of honor eventually prevailed and dissuaded me at the last moment from completing the sabotage. But that would be substituting one lie for another. It was not honor that intervened, but a sudden change of wind. I was within seconds of wrecking *Dove* and abandoning her to the ocean bottom when the wind backed to the north and then to the northeast—a freak and sudden change I'd never experienced on this coast before. The sails filled at once and white water spewed from *Dove*'s southwest-bound bow.

I have not before told anyone about this sabotage plan which failed. It is hard enough to confess it now. I do so only because I now believe that nature's intervention was designed, related in a way (that some will understand and others cynically reject) to the sudden calming of the sea that saved my life in the great storm off Malagasy.

So through a freak wind (or special blessing) I made the journey to Plettenbergbaai and because there were no docking facilities I anchored Dove two hundred yards off the boiling surf. I searched the beach through my binoculars and in a moment focused on a young girl standing quite alone, a girl in blue jeans, her hands shielding her eyes against the glare, her wheaten hair streaming in the wind.

From the beach Patti watched me launch Dove's small dinghy and paddle shoreward. She saw the swell gather up and arc behind me and then catch the dinghy in its crest. The dinghy somersaulted and as I was hurled into the surf Patti ran to the water's edge and helped pull me up the beach—a soaked and shivering and very lucky sailor. We salvaged the dinghy too.

"And now," I said as I gasped for air, "what about some mouth-to-mouth resuscitation?"

Patti had found a small room overlooking the bay of this small and beautiful resort. She undressed me and dried me down, but I have no memory of going to bed. I slept for eighteen hours straight and was awakened by a furious pounding on the bedroom door.

Some Cape Colored fishermen had come to tell me that Dove was dragging and would soon be on the rocks. On arriving at Plet (as the locals call it) I had expected the onshore gale and had put out enough chain and line to give two anchors four hundred feet of scope. But against a raging sea this anchorage was not enough.

Still buttoning my pants, I reached the beach. Dove was clearly in the gravest peril. The fishermen gathered around and gave me advice. Even their sturdy powered boats could not cope with the thundering breakers.

The boat I had planned to wreck three days earlier was now about to destroy itself unless I could do something about it in a hurry.

The one hope was to swim through the angry surf. The sea felt cold enough for ice floes and it took me fifteen minutes and all my strength to reach *Dove's* rolling gunwale. For a while I simply clung to the side, unable to muster the extra energy to heave myself aboard. Realizing that I would soon simply freeze to death, I found a reserve of strength to scramble to the deck.

One of the two anchor lines had parted, which was why *Dove* was dragging. The other three-quarter-inch nylon was stretching like a rubber band. If this snapped, as it could do at any moment, the whiplash would make fishbait of my entrails. I went below and got out my big anchor and gave it all the chain I had. The wind was howling like a hundred jackals. A diver in a wetsuit swam out to help. Between us we were able to set *Dove's* heaviest ground tackle.

There wasn't anything else to do. *Dove* would have to battle out the storm alone. I gave her little hope, and I filled a plastic bag with all my important papers and my money (about one hundred dollars), tied a life preserver around my chest and dived overboard. Without the life preserver I wouldn't have made the shore.

Once again Patti dried me off, and she massaged my back, which I'd strained when carrying the heavy anchor across a heaving deck. This time I could not sleep, because I worried about *Dove* fighting for her life.

The storm lasted two full days and nights, but the anchors held. When I swam out to *Dove* again I was really proud of her. The boat had a courage of her own and, wounded though she was (the anchor's rope had ripped away five feet of toe rail), she had come through without my help. The decks were again leaking where they joined the hull. The cabin was a mess. My little radio looked as if it had been a monkey's toy.

While the wind remained in the wrong quarter there was a chance to see this stretch of coast and make friends with the Colored fishermen. On Saturday night they drank themselves under the table, but on Sunday, dressed in starched shirts, their women in flowered hats, they took us to their little whitewashed church. I was surprised to find that all races worshiped here together. They seemed to forget for an hour or so each week the apartheid which causes so much bitterness.

We found kindness everywhere. A group of white women had organized a nonprofit store where the poorest Coloreds could buy staple foods for prices well within their budgets. But the poorest Afrikaners were too proud to buy there. Some politicians had told them they should not mix with those who had darker skins. It was crazy to see how racial issues had been used by the politicians. It seemed to us that unless all South Africans, black, white and brown, began to see each other as fellowmen with common needs, there'd be real danger of bloodshed in their lovely land.

The bell of the little whitewashed church was calling the faithful to the Easter Sunday service on the day I sailed again—this time only forty miles to Knysna. The entrance to Knysna harbor is one of the loveliest in the world and, with its narrow, rocky gateway and huge swells, one of the most dangerous. Patti had arrived ahead of me on Elsa. Next day we hitched a ride to Cape Town to see if there was any mail. There was, and among the letters was one from my parents saying they had had second thoughts about my marrying Patti.

It didn't matter now because except for "that little piece of paper" we had been man and wife for several months.

Leaving Knysna on April 25 remains one of the special memories of my voyage. Patti had climbed high up on the cliffs overlooking the narrow harbor entrance. She waved down to me four hundred feet below. She had become a good photographer and from her high position took one of the best pictures of *Dove*, showing the tiny craft against a great rampart of rocks and heading for the open sea.

It always hurt so much to leave Patti behind. We weren't like an American suburban couple kissing on the doorstep before the husband joins the snake of traffic to his downtown office and the wife returns to her kitchen to wash up the breakfast things. With us there was always the chance of not seeing each other again. I don't want to overplay the danger, but sailing along the South African coast against the prevailing wind and in a season when storms blow up in minutes wasn't, as they put it in South Africa, "everyone's cup of tea." The headlands here and hidden rocks have wrecked a fleet of ships, ranging from great ocean liners to boats as small as Dove. Few coastlines in the world have more stories of disaster—and of heroism too. I had just been reading the account of the sinking of the Birkenhead, one of the most stirring of all the tales of the sea.

In 1852, not far from where Dove was now sailing, the Birkenhead, an iron paddle steamer of about two thousand tons, had struck the pinnacle of rock called Danger Point. The rock ripped her hull and in twenty minutes she broke in two and sank. Of the 638 aboard, mostly young British soldiers going to the Kaffir Wars, only 184 were saved. The Birkenhead disaster is remembered because every woman and child was saved. The men stood on the deck in line, knowing that most of them were going to drown, while the women and children filled the boats. Copies of Thomas Hemy's famous Birkenhead picture of a boy drummer beating a final salute to his comrades was hung in the nurseries of Victorian England and children were told that this was the discipline and courage which had created the British Empire.

Each time I went to sea now it was not for myself I feared. I worried what Patti would do if Dove simply failed to turn up at the next port. Dove wasn't really seaworthy any longer, and a storm could quickly find her weakness—especially at the places where the deck had separated from the hull. A big wave could crush the deck like cardboard. If this were to happen she would sink in seconds.

My plan on sailing out from Knysna was to slip around the southernmost point of Africa, Cape Agulhas (many people wrongly think that the Cape of Good Hope is the southernmost point). Once around Agulhas, the return to California would be, as I told my tape, "all downhill."

Patti rode the motorcycle to Gordon's Bay. I told her to watch out for me in three days. My first few miles in Dove proved easy sailing. The wind was on the port quarter. But the second day out the wind came around to the southwest again. By tacking I managed to make eighty-three miles in three days.

I told the tape recorder: *Oh, man! This is absolutely stupid! I've made thirteen miles in the last thirteen hours!*

I pulled into Stilbaai, which is sheltered from the west, to take some sleep. Next morning I tried once again to beat into the wind. That night I could see the lights of Cape Agulhas, still forty-four miles away, bouncing off the bottoms of low clouds, then at dawn the radio crackled a gale warning.

This was what I most feared. I scooted into Struisbaai, just short of Cape Agulhas, and dropped anchor in the nick of time. An absolute fury of a wind roared and wailed about my head for a full week, and although bare-poled *Dove* was protected by the land, she pitched and rolled, and even at anchor was taking quite a beating. Now I was short of food and the huge breakers hitting the coast made it impossible to get ashore in my six-foot dinghy. Actually there was a real danger of the anchor line parting and of *Dove* being blown out to sea.

Into the tape recorder I protested: *Wouldn't be surprised if the whole stupid boat doesn't simply fall apart any minute. . . . Just lost my coffee pot over the side and I am trying to make some more by boiling percolator coffee in a pan. It tastes like sand. At least it's warm. . . . My good food is all gone and I'll have to eat from the rusty cans left over from the Solomons. . . . Oh, man, what a bore this is! Patti must be really worried. . . . Just had some awful soup and will probably get ptomaine or something. I'm just existing. . . .*

A fishing boat riding out the storm with *Dove* came up alongside and the skipper generously threw me a fish. The change of diet helped boost my morale. To pass the time I began to make a pair of leather sandals for Patti.

On the eleventh day after leaving Knysna a red-painted aircraft dipped overhead, and toward evening of that day the sound of voices brought me up on deck. Another fishing boat was alongside. Shouting into the wind, the skipper asked, "Where's your wife?"

I'd run out of both humor and old groceries. "What business is it of yours? She's in Gordon's Bay," I yelled.

The skipper grinned as Patti appeared on the fishing boat's deck. "Oh, no I'm not," she laughed.

When Patti had arrived in Gordon's Bay she'd guessed I'd been delayed by bad weather, but when ten days had passed without any word of me she was really troubled. She had thought of riding back down the coast to look for a sail or wreckage and was about to set off when the associate editor of *National Geographic*, Gilbert Grosvenor, turned up at Gordon's Bay. He had come from Washington to help me revise my first story for the magazine.

Gil had heard that we were married. When he was looking for me someone had casually spoken of Mrs. Graham. This surprised him. Patti did not want to create another scene like the one in Darwin so she thought it was best to tell him the full story. Patti thought Gil looked like the kind of person who would understand and besides she was so concerned about my safety that she felt he might be helpful in finding out where I was.

Gil did understand our situation very well and was quite satisfied when Patti told him that I planned to continue my voyage single-handed. In fact he suggested that the *National Geographic* articles would gain by the inclusion of a piece about my falling in love with a California girl. But he was worried as well that I had apparently vanished in the week-long storm and he immediately arranged for a search plane to scour the coastline. This was the red-colored aircraft I'd seen. The pilot had spotted me and reported back to Patti and Gil that I was holed out in Struisbaai. Gil then rented a car and brought Patti down the coast for our unexpected and marvelous reunion.

Pretty soon after Patti had turned up on the fishing boat the storm died down and we all went ashore. We stayed in a small hotel and for the next five days Gil and I revised the manuscript.

Then I returned to *Dove* and, running before a fresh easterly, sailed around Africa's southernmost tip and anchored within the breakwater of Gordon's Bay.

We were to spend two months here, readying *Dove* for the transatlantic voyage. With the cooperation of the friendly port captain, Major Douglas van Riet, we got *Dove* up on the ways.

The return of *Dove* in Fort Lauderdale, Florida—the thirty-three-foot fiberglass sloop I finished the voyage in, after selling little *Dove* in the Virgin Islands.

Getting big *Dove* ready for sea.

Running before the wind out of Virgin Gorda Sound, *Dove* rigged with double headsails set wing and wing. (*Patricia Graham*)

Near Nassau on the way from Florida to the Virgin Islands.

From the Bahamas to St. Thomas.

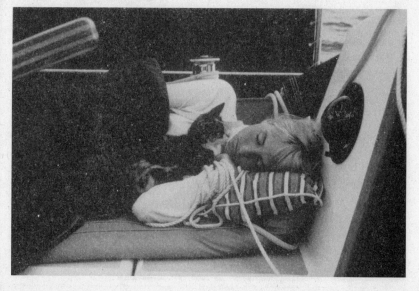

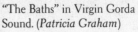
"The Baths" in Virgin Gorda
Sound. (*Patricia Graham*)

Head carpenter, and the only one,
Bitter End Resort, Virgin Gorda
Sound.

Virgin Gorda Sound.

Grouper speared during lunch break, Virgin Gorda Sound.

En route from the Virgin Islands to the San Blas Islands near Panama.

From Panama, I sailed *Dove* to San Cristobal in the Galapagos Islands 700 miles west of the South American coast.

Giant tortoise, Galapagos Islands.

Fernandina sea lion.

Marine Iguana.

Mockingbird on Hood island.

Galapagos Islands, lobster, and Robin.

Tagus Cove.

Baby sea lion on Hood island.

Baby booby—Hood island.

Isabela penguin.

In the doldrums.

Slicing homemade bread.

Off San Clemente, California, about a day's sail from home.

Cooling off and keeping clean with rainwater I caught in the mainsail.

Sighting the breakwaters of Los Angeles harbor, April 30, 1970.

Welcome home. (*L. Graham*).

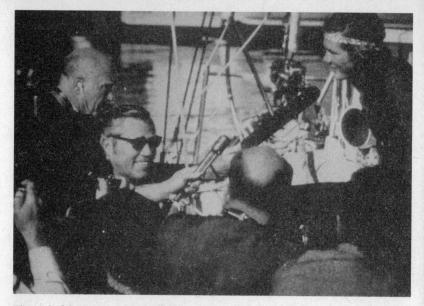

The end of the voyage is now official.

Quimby in her bathtub at
Long Beach Marina.

Patti coming out to greet my arrival home.

Patti and Quimby, Patrick Creek, settling in.

Patti, Quimby, and I taking a break. We are building our log house (tool shed in the background) and hope to grow or make most of the things we need. (*Derek Gill*)

Montana, 1971. We've decided to live here in the mountains, learning from nature how we are meant to live. (*Patricia Graham*)

Patrick Creek cabin, Quimby and Robin.

Technicians from Cape Town helped me fiberglass the deck to the hull and to paint the boat from stem to stern. Dove looked respectable again—and safe.

Gordon's Bay is a small resort, with cottages built of local stone and fringed by lawns. Usually Patti and I slept on Dove, but our second home was Thelma's boardinghouse, where we took our meals. Most of the residents at Thelma's were retired people, old enough to be our grandparents. We got to know them well, often playing canasta with them in the evenings. One man of eighty-five taught me how to crochet, and his wife, perhaps ten years younger, knitted me a sweater. They held hands and looked at each other like a young couple on a honeymoon.

"Is that what love's all about?" asked Patti, half seriously as we strolled back to Dove one evening. "I mean, two old people holding hands?"

It was partly the married bliss of this old couple that made us think of our own marriage once again—or at least of making it legal.

When we returned to the cabin, where Patti bundled herself up in a blanket against the cold, we talked about my parents' belated consent to our marriage.

"Maybe we should make it legal," I said. "After all, I still have to explain you to people. That makes me sick."

"You prefer a wife to a mistress?" asked Patti, her eyes laughing above the blanket.

"Mistress is a word which always makes me think of dirty old men," I protested.

Patti was suddenly serious. "Robin, perhaps what's important is not the marriage certificate. But supposing we have children? Could happen, you know." She paused and then added, "Let's never hurt anyone deliberately, not your parents, not anyone."

That's what made us decide to go to the magistrate's office at Hermanus Bay next morning. There I handed over my parents' written consent to a severe-looking woman with black hair and a sallow skin.

The woman snapped, "When do you want to get married?"

"Today," I said.

The woman looked us up and down critically, taking in my shoulder-length hair, our baggy sweaters, sea-stained jeans and bare feet. She pressed her lips together in disapproval.

"You'll need a hat," she told Patti, "and we need twenty-four hours' notice of a marriage. The magistrate has other duties too. You'll also need a special license, which costs ten rand [fourteen dollars]."

I handed over a ten-rand bill. "Okay, we'll be here at eleven o'clock tomorrow," I said.

The woman did not smile.

On leaving the magistrate's court I said to Patti, "Let's find a honeymoon hotel." We rode Elsa a little up the coast and found the perfect place—the Birkenhead Hotel. It was named for the ship which went down heroically. As it was out of season, the hotel proprietor invited us to choose our own room. Like kids we dashed about the corridors, opening doors, testing the views and bedsprings. Then, in a corner of the second floor, we found a room so right that it seemed made for us. One huge window looked out across the sea and the other gave a view of the magnificent Hottentots Holland Mountains and a broad sweep of vineyards in the valley.

"Well, which room have you chosen?" asked the girl behind the desk. We told her the number and she smiled, "Oh, that's our special bridal suite," she said.

Next day we returned to the magistrate's office, dressed in our most formal clothes. I was wearing my only jacket and had found a crumpled tie under the canned goods. I discovered too, my Darwin shoes—the ones with copper-wire laces. Patti put on an attractive dress but she had no hat so I lent her my watch cap. The magistrate was a cheerful and pink-cheeked Afrikaner. He put on his black robe and asked two of the girl clerks to come into his office and be witnesses.

We stood there holding hands. At the key point of the short ceremony the magistrate asked me for the ring. Of course, I'd forgotten about that, but Patti pulled the Durban ring off her finger and gave it to me. I returned it to her finger and then we kissed. I think we kissed a bit too early because the magistrate cleared his throat. Everyone signed their names on the certificate. Even the woman with black hair gave us a sort of smile.

Outside the office, I turned to Patti and asked, "Do you feel any different now?"

She laughed. "No different from when we married ourselves."

Then Mr. and Mrs. Robin Lee Graham (officially) mounted their ancient motorcycle and drove off to their honeymoon hotel.

It was the Cape's midwinter and pretty cold, but at the hotel we thawed out in front of a huge log fire. When we went to the bridal suite we found hot water bottles between the sheets.

In its own way our second wedding was pretty neat too.

~~~ 8

The Third Quarter

CROSSING THE ATLANTIC from Cape Town may be "all downhill," as I had told the tape recorder, but it's a very long hill. I figured it was five thousand miles to the north coast of South America.

Concerned for my safety, *National Geographic* had given me an expensive piece of additional equipment—a two-way radio. When this was installed Patti helped me provision *Dove* with $120 worth of canned goods. She was careful to include special things we'd enjoyed together: artichoke hearts, sour cream mix, canned oysters and pickled fish—especially pickled fish.

At Gordon's Bay, Harbor Master van Riet, who loved animals as much as the sea, gave us two kittens, one orange and the other tortoise shell. We named them Kili and Fili, for the youngest dwarfs in J. R. R. Tolkien's *Hobbit* book, which we had read aloud to each other in *Dove's* cabin. The kittens were born with bad eyes and I don't think anyone else would have wanted them. We'd taken them to an animal hospital where in spite of skillful surgery Fili lost her sight completely.

There was no room on *Dove* for the motorcycle, Elsa, which had served us faithfully, so we gave it to Thelma's son. The old people at the boardinghouse came down to the harbor to say good-bye. Their arms were filled with fresh fruit, candy and knitted things. Patti and I were really touched by their kindness and farewells. I don't know how to explain it, but we have a special feeling for old people.

When the radio was fixed up it was just a question of waiting in Cape Town for a fair wind—a wind from the south. We counted each of these last days together and we never spoke of the time when we'd have to go our separate ways.

In Darwin Patti had bought a ticket to the Canary Islands, off Spain, at a very low immigrant's fare. Patti had had a specially frustrating day when the shipping people at Cape Town told her that her ticket was outdated. She burst into tears—a rare thing for Patti to do. One of the men at the shipping office lent her his handkerchief and said he would do what he could to help her. Anyway, they stretched a point and fixed her up without extra charge in a three-berth cabin on the Italian liner *Europa*.

The *Europa* was bound for Barcelona, and Patti now had enough cash for a trip through Europe before sailing to join me in Surinam, (Dutch Guiana). At least, that was the plan. It was a question of who'd sail first.

On Saturday morning, July 13, we were walking along a beach with massive Table Mountain in the background when Patti's hand suddenly tightened in my own. I followed her eyes to the land side of the beach.

"Look at the trees," she said quietly.

The shorefront trees were bending to the wind. For the first time in two weeks they were bending to the north.

Two hours later I was sailing *Dove* out of Cape Town's harbor. I'd left in such a hurry that Patti had not had time to get all her stuff off *Dove*. But she did take my only comb and pen. Across the Atlantic I tried to control my hair with a primitive Fijian wooden comb and had to write up my logbook in pencil. I could find no use for her toothbrush, her bikini pants or her lipstick.

Patti followed me out for a few miles in a friend's powerboat. When her boat turned around she blew kisses across the water. Thank God she couldn't see me cry.

My first logbook entry read: *Damn it! Damn it! How I hate to leave!*

The *Europa* was due to sail from the Cape in three days, and with the liner's radio officer I'd arranged for a schedule of times when Patti and I could speak to each other on my new radiotelephone. We'd figured out where *Dove* and the *Europa* would be close enough for good reception. This scheduled radio talk was something to look forward to.

Those first days out of Cape Town there was much to keep me busy. I had to watch for shipping heading north and south in one of the busiest shipping lanes in the world. This meant staying up all night every night for the first week. In daylight, when I slept, I hoped *Dove* would be seen by the steamers and that they would give way to sail. A radar reflector on *Dove*'s mast should show up on a steamer's screen. In the first six days I counted fifty-four ships, some so close that they rocked *Dove* in their wash.

To pass the time I began to crochet a Balaklava helmet to protect my face against the cold. The wind seemed to be coming right out of the South Pole, and when spray came over the bow and swept across the deck it took my breath away.

My first call to Patti was due on July 17 at seven in the morning, and I figured that if the *Europa* had left on time she would be only about two hundred miles away. The previous night I'd written down all the things I had wanted to say. As the hour approached I was so tensed up I couldn't force myself to eat and at exactly 0700 hours I turned on my transmitter and spoke into the microphone:

"Yacht *Dove* calling *Europa*. *Dove* calling *Europa*."

Silence.

"*Dove* calling *Europa*."

Suddenly the radio crackled, "*Europa* motor vessel calling yacht *Dove*."

Then Patti came through loud and clear. But from the way she spoke it was obvious she wasn't hearing me. She said, "Robin, where are you, honey?"

I called back desperately, "I hear you, Patti; what's the matter? Why can't you pick me up?"

Silence again, then *Europa's* radioman cut in and told me to call on another frequency. Frantically I fiddled with the dial, but my radio did not have the frequency he'd asked for. I spent an hour trying to make contact. Finally the *Europa* said they would call again in two hours.

At 0900 *Europa* picked up my call. It was fantastic to hear Patti. I'd lost the piece of paper on which I'd written the carefully thought out messages, so we talked about the weather and the cats. Then Patti said, "They tell me you're only about 140 miles away."

"Close enough to swim," I said.

"Okay," said Patti. "I'll start swimming too. That's only seventy miles for each of us. In case you don't recognize me I'll be wearing my red bikini."

"Without your pants," I said. "You left them in the quarter bunk locker."

"Okay, without my pants."

The radioman interrupted to warn that we were speaking on an emergency frequency and that we'd be in trouble if we spoke longer. He promised to make contact again that night.

I told my tape recorder: *Just had a long really nice talk with Patti. Gee, it was nice. I really feel good now. I'm so happy I even sing a little. This call was worth all the work and the cost that went into this radio. . . . I love her very much.*

We had another long talk that night but next morning when we again made ship-to-ship contact Patti's voice was unintelligible. It was the last time I heard her on this leg of the voyage.

The kittens were good company. For hours I would watch them playing with each other, clawing at everything that moved, tumbling into their food. I taped: *Fili, the blind one, jumps at Kili and misses by a cat's length. She bumps into the bulkhead all the time,* but even though she's sightless she never messes outside the litter box. Kili's eyes are troubling him too. I've just been doctoring him and with some tweezers I've plucked the inward-growing eyelashes from his eyes.

Man, it was cold! I had built a cozy bunk under the poop deck in the area where the cockpit had been. Patti had dubbed this spot "the cave," and although I couldn't sit up there inside the cave, it was a warm spot and it gave me a sense of security. I spent a lot of time reading in the cave or simply thinking about the future.

After a week at sea, and eight hundred miles from Cape Town, the shipping traffic thinned, then disappeared. On my ninth day at sea, Dove's sails filled with the southeast trades and I put out a jib and a genoa on whisker poles.

On July 27 I taped: *Have gone three years from this date, but it seems like half my lifetime. . . . Last night I put up the man-overboard light, which really floodlit the sails and deck. Felt it safe to take a seven-hour sleep. Self-steering gear working perfectly. Weather has begun to warm up too and I've been able to discard my sweater and read again on deck. . . . Cats are always hungry but I find eating is a drag—even the special food that Patti bought me. Last night I tried some pickled fish, but it reminded me so much of being with Patti in South Africa that I cried like a baby. I couldn't bear to eat the stuff and threw it overboard. . . . Loneliness is like a pain again.*

Next day I recorded: *This morning I saw a brilliant orange thing floating in the water. I moved Dove over and scooped up a Japanese net float. Two crabs were clinging to it. I knew they would die if I flung them back into the water. The sea is a mile deep here and the pressure down below would soon kill them. I gave the crabs a rest on Dove's stern and then made a miniature raft from the styrofoam top to my ice chest. I hollowed out the little raft and provisioned it with barnacles and then put the crabs aboard. I've just watched the little raft floating off behind me. I hope the barnacles will keep the crabs from starvation until they make it to a shoreline.*

The radio was important to me now. Although I could not talk to anyone I could listen to other ships talking to each other. A friend in South Africa had given me a collection of taped folk songs, but all I wanted to hear was a live human voice. I picked up the BBC overseas broadcasts and more rarely the Voice of America. I even enjoyed the commercials because they made me feel closer to people. When I couldn't find an English broadcast I listened to people speaking in languages I couldn't understand. I taped: *At least I know there are other people around.*

In the monotony of these days the little things seemed big. With the care of a watchmaker I worked out a special plumbing arrangement for the cats, shaping two pans and perforating the smaller one, which carried the litter. All I had to do to keep the cats' bathroom reasonably clean was to empty the bottom pan and wash it out over the side.

As the days passed, my reflexes slowed down. I now spent twice as long taking a sun fix and working out my position. My tape recorder gives an idea of my mood: *I lost my chronometer today and I panicked when I couldn't find it. I can't navigate without it. Then I found it among the food stores. I don't know why I put it there. . . .*

One afternoon when I was filling the canvas bucket with sea-water before taking a bath, the handle broke and the bucket floated away aft. I needed that bucket, but it took me several minutes to find the initiative and energy to turn *Dove* around and beat to windward to retrieve it. The maneuver cost me my supper of dried fish. The strips of fish had been drying on the deck, but when I beat back to windward, heeling sharply, the fish slid into the water. I got the bucket back though.

Saint Helena, where Napoleon had died, hove into sight on July 31. I was tempted to explore the island but knew that to do so would cost me a day or more, so I sailed on to Ascension, 635 miles to the north northwest. I taped: *I'm not eager to go to Ascension. I'm just going there to get provisions. As each day passes I get a little more depressed and lonely.*

About halfway between the two islands I fell overboard. My fishing line had become entangled with the outboard shaft and in trying to get it free I lost my balance. *Dove* was moving at about five knots, but I was just able to grab the stern pulpit. Although I was wearing a safety harness I might not have been able to haul myself back on board at that speed.

On this voyage across the Atlantic I read a lot. The book I enjoyed the most in a library that included detective stories, travel books and historical novels was Lloyd Douglas's *The Robe*. It made me wonder if there was some sort of purpose to my life. Like many people of my age, I had dismissed God and religion "and all that stuff" as something packaged up with stained-glass windows, dreary organ music and an old man with a beard. *The Robe* kind of shook me up. It's the story of the centurion who watched Jesus die and who won his robe in a lottery.

After twenty-three days at sea I dropped anchor in Ascension island's Clarence Bay. With its moonlike landscape dotted with electronic antennae and the "big dishes" of deep-space-tracking stations, the island looked right out of science fiction.

As it was late in the evening, and too late to go ashore, I started to fish and at once hooked a good-size bonita. While the fish was still hanging over *Dove's* side a hammerhead shark snapped it clean in half. When the hammerhead came back for second helpings I shot it through the head, but in case he had any brothers I decided against a swim.

Next morning I pulled ashore in the dinghy and was given a ride to the Air Force base. The people there had heard about me and gave me red carpet treatment. This was rather embarrassing as I did not possess a pair of shoes (I'd thrown away the ones with copper laces) and, after so long at sea, I just couldn't carry on a proper conversation. I think the Air Force people thought I was Dopey. It was good, though, to eat inch-thick steak again.

I was so glad to get news of Patti and that she had arrived safely in Europe. Her cable said: "Still hoping to see you Surinam on time. Love you."

One of the technicians took me on a tour of the island. I was much more excited to discover a dump of ancient grog bottles—the relics of a seafarers' party long ago—than I was with all the scientific apparatus which tracked the hardware up in space. I really wanted to be on my way again because Patti would cross the Atlantic a lot quicker than *Dove*. I stocked up with fresh milk, fresh vegetables and ice and set sail again on August 16.

These sailing days had a basic routine. I would usually go to sleep at midnight and wake when the sun was fifteen degrees above the horizon—a good time to take a first sun fix and cook some breakfast. Then I would check *Dove's* mileage over the twenty-four-hour period and figure out how long it would take me to the next landfall—in this instance Paramaribo in Surinam. If I'd made good progress I was happy; if I hadn't I was depressed. Then I would sit on deck in the morning sun, collecting an all-over tan, and daydream or read. At noon I would get my LOP and, if I was hungry, eat again and feed the cats. I preferred to plot my position on the larger charts because my penciled markings showed up as a bigger movement across the ocean. In the afternoon I would read again and take a seawater bucket bath. I didn't have any salt water soap so I didn't lather up. But the bath was always a high point of the day because it was so refreshing, and there was no shortage of bathwater.

Evening was the time I liked best. Then I would listen to the BBC or the Voice of America and watch the sun set. I felt especially close to Patti in the evenings. If my sailing distance had proved disappointing I'd go to bed early. Depending on the movement of the boat I would sleep curled up forward on the floor of the cabin or in the cave.

The best thing about the cave was its contrast to the vastness of the sky. The head shrinkers would probably tell me I wanted to return to the womb or something.

I explained this routine on my tape recorder and said: *You just look at the progress you make each day, hoping to get a little further, which you do most of the time. . . . I haven't used much of the stuff aboard that has to be cooked. It's just a waste of time to cook when you can't enjoy it. I'd rather heat up a can.*

Because of constant trade winds and the east-west current, I generally made good distances on this long leg of the voyage. On August 23—my eleventh day out of Ascension—the taffrail log checked 129 miles but my LOP showed *Dove* had covered 177 miles over the bottom. The record was broken again on August 30, with a true distance of 185 miles. I rarely had to change sails, the two jibs, wing and wing, bowling *Dove* along at her best speed.

On my fifteenth day at sea I taped: *Just caught a twenty-pound barracuda . . . the cats liked it too. . . . Listening to a Spanish program and don't understand a word. The newscaster sounds excited about something. Am now on the equator and it's really hot —always hotter in the morning than in the afternoon. Dove's in a mess. It's amazing what a mess a little boat can get into! House-cleaning keeps me busy. Every day I've got to fight the loneliness of this voyage. It's a slow torture, not like the sudden fear you get in a storm, but more like a bad toothache. I'm never really free of it.*

Blind Fili's courage amazed me. She knew her way about the boat, though if I moved any piece of gear out of its usual position she would bump into it—but only once. Next time around she would take evasive action.

Unlike her sighted brother, the blind kitten padded about *Dove* with her whiskers forward like radio antennae. She knew just how close to walk to the edge of the deck, sensing the danger even when chasing Kili. Sightless Fili was more independent than Kili, who would come to my lap and purr, demanding affection and approval. But Fili would move away when I stroked her back.

Perhaps, I reflected into the tape, *blind creatures, human or animal, have their own pride, and prefer bruises to dependence on another creature. They are good company, these kittens.*

On August 30 I saw the first sign of human life in eighteen days. A Brazilian schooner moved across my port beam. She was sailing wing and wing and looked like a huge white butterfly on the water. When she came close I saw she was aptly called *Grace.*

At midnight on the thirty-first I spotted the lightship at the mouth of the Suriname River and at dawn I was sailing *Dove* upstream toward Paramaribo. In the evening I anchored off what appeared to be the town's main square, hoping that this was the place where Patti would be most likely to find me. Next morning I cleared customs and made for the post office, where the clerk said there was no mail for me at all.

Back on *Dove* I taped: *I knew there must be mail. I could have punched the guy on the nose. That wouldn't have helped though. I'm just so depressed.*

A hostile customs officer came aboard and poked about for contraband and then told me the district commissioner wanted to see me immediately. I could think of no crime I'd committed on the high seas in the forty-four days it had taken me to sail from Cape Town. Anyway all was well: the commissioner, Mr. Frits Barend, had collected my mail for me—including ten letters from Patti.

Patti had spent six weeks in Europe, visiting friends in Switzerland and England. One letter read:

Europe is so lovely, so different. But you weren't here with me, Robin, and traveling without you is so pointless, so flat, too often just plain boring. I would look up at a Swiss mountain, snow-covered and lovely against a blue sky. I wanted to point to the peak and to find you at my shoulder and tell you all about it.

It was the same in lovely England. Oh, those gentle colors, those thatch-roofed villages, duck ponds and village greens and the gray, old cities full of history with little shops and everyone traveling on the wrong side of the road.

From a train window I saw the green, green fields and hedgerows and a little girl riding a bicycle down a country road. And I thought, this is it. This is England! It was how I imagined it, only better. But you weren't here, Robin. You weren't sitting across the corner of the car. And when I looked again it was all so ordinary, so dreary without you. One day you and I will have to come back and see England again. We'll ride on a motorcycle like we did in South

Africa. It'll all be quite different, all so perfect. I know now what you mean when you say traveling alone is for the birds. It's funny how traveling used to be great when I was single. But when you are married and alone it's not fun at all.

I read her letters in sequence, carefully sorting them in order from their dates, and I tried to picture her walking through the hot boulevards of Barcelona, sipping coffee on a veranda overlooking the Lake of Geneva, picking strawberries in an English country garden or looking up at Eros in Piccadilly. I tried to see Patti swinging her slim brown legs along a cobbled street or throwing darts in a low-beamed English pub. I tried to imagine her laughing or sitting alone and sad on a park bench with kids playing on the swings.

Her last letter reported that she had returned to Barcelona hoping to find a ship sailing directly for Surinam, but the best she could do was to get a ship for the Caribbean. She gave a Trinidad address—the home of friends. I sent a cable to await her arrival. The cable read: "Take supersonic plane or satellite for Paramaribo."

The district commissioner offered to show me a bit of his country, but I was worried that Patti might arrive and find me gone. Only when Mr. Barend had promised that he would have Patti flown directly into the interior to join me did I agree to go with him.

Along with a free-lance photographer, Mr. Barend took me fishing on a huge man-made lake created by damming up the Suriname River. We caught a sackful of piranhas, the vicious fish that can strip a human body to its bones in minutes. They were surprisingly good to eat. Then we took a small plane to Paloemeu and sailed an outboard dugout canoe up the Tapanahoni River to an Indian mission station in the village of Tepoe. The Indians were really hospitable. They let me sleep in the thatched hut of a family absent from the village. The village boys showed me what good marksmen they were with their bows. The missionaries had not, as others had in other places, forced western dress and customs on the natives. Even when the Indians went to church they wore only a tiny covering fore and aft. They still hunted game with bows and arrows. I swam in rapids after being promised three times that piranhas don't live in fast-moving water.

One of the priests gave me a green parrot. The bird had grown up in the cloisters, so it did not know a single oath. I was standing on a jungle airstrip with the parrot on my shoulder when Patti's small plane flew in. The plane's door shot open and Patti jumped out looking gorgeous.

As we ran to each other the parrot screeched in alarm and flew back to the mission station. Anyway, we did not need any company, feathered or in priestly gowns, when we held each other for the first time in two months—to the day.

Patti had started keeping a diary again, and the entry for the day we were reunited reads: "Robin's nerves seem shot to pieces. The Atlantic crossing has really bugged him. He wants to end the voyage here and has written to his father and National Geographic saying he is not going to sail alone again."

These letters had fast results. Gil Grosvenor flew out from Washington to persuade me to complete the voyage alone. Both Patti and I liked Gil, and I hope he has forgiven me for the way I treated him. I wasn't ready to listen to reason, but I really wanted to tell him, "Look Gil, I'm not like this at all. It's just that I'm uptight now. I know you've come an awful long way and I know that you're an understanding guy. But can't you see that I'm finished, that I can't stand going it alone any more? Just give me time and I'll be myself again. Next time we meet I'll be quite different, you'll see. I'll slap your back and keep my cool. But not now, please not now."

I didn't say anything like that. Over dinner in Paramaribo's best hotel I told Gil that I'd rather face a tank of hungry piranhas than put to sea alone again.

I told him, "I hate that bloody boat. I know her every creak, every bubble of her blistered paint. I know exactly how she'll behave in every wind and every wave.

"Besides," I added, "*Dove*'s no longer safe. I've lost confidence in her. I don't trust her any more."

Gil quietly suggested that *National Geographic* might help me buy a bigger boat with advance royalties. The offer sank into my mind just before I drank myself to sleep. Next day Gil flew out, convinced of the failure of his mission.

Of course time is a healer, even when you're sitting in a small boat on a dirty river. Patti nursed me back to mental health. These must have been wretched days for her as we lived through them on *Dove*. We sailed to Paranam, the huge bauxite plant upriver from Paramaribo. Red dust was everywhere, staining the houses of the miners, the vegetation and the water—a real James Bond setting in the jungle.

When we'd tied *Dove* to a wharf we went to sleep. No one had told us about the ten-foot tide. At midnight we were suddenly thrown from our bunks as *Dove* fell over onto her side. The outgoing tide had left *Dove* precariously balanced on her keel, and perhaps one of us coughed or stirred in our sleep and upset the balance. Anyway, after the first shock of believing we'd been hit by an earthquake, we lay down across the portholes and roared with laughter. This was the turning point of my mental slide.

The days were happier now. We'd usually go to the Paramaribo market to bargain for food, and find ourselves bidding against Indians and bush Negroes, blacks, whites, Chinese—I'd never come across such a mixup of races. They laughed at me because I was barefooted. The Negroes had been imported to work the canefields, but Surinam was one of the first countries to free the slaves. Most of the Negroes had stayed on. The Surinam flag carries five colors, representing the five different skin colors of the people.

Dove was too small for the two of us. We couldn't even stand up straight in the cabin. It was like living in a bathroom with nowhere to put my shaving things. Gil Grosvenor's suggestion of a bigger boat to complete the voyage began to look more attractive. I put a call through to Washington and spoke to Charles Allmon of the NG staff, who liked my idea that I sail *Dove* to Barbados and from there negotiate for a bigger boat.

I pulled out my atlas. "I suppose California isn't all that far," I told Patti. I had sailed 22,000 miles and three-quarters of the way around the world. The last quarter didn't look too bad.

Patti said quietly, "I believe you're meant to finish what you set out to do."

"And prove the world is round?" I snapped.

"And prove something important to yourself," she said.

We made plans to leave. I would sail to Barbados and Patti would take a boat to Trinidad and then fly over to join me.

On October 12 I powered out to the lightship at the mouth of the Suriname River and waited for Patti's steamer, a bauxite boat, to catch up. As the steamer passed me and made for the open sea I was attacked by another bout of anger and frustration. I hated to set sail alone again. As Patti waved good-bye from the after rail I got so mad I smashed one of the whisker poles against the mast.

Then the pilot boat came alongside and a man in a peaked cap told me to turn on my radio. I went below and switched it to the frequency the pilot had given me. Patti was on the air.

She guessed what I was going through and said, "Remember, Robin, it's the last time on the little boat, and really it's a very short sail."

"I'm going to be miserable." I said.

"No, no," said Patti, "don't feel like that. I'll be thinking about you all the time and at six every morning I'll be thinking about you really hard. You do the same at six o'clock and we'll sort of talk to each other."

"Okay, I'll do that. I'll try," I said.

"I'm sure it'll work, you'll see. Remember that old man who crossed the Pacific in a raft and how he talked to his wife thousands of miles away."

"Yeah, I remember."

"And Robin."

"Yes?"

"I love you very much."

Then there was silence again.

~~ 9

Bigger Wings and Baby Talk

AT BARBADOS we were lucky to find a neat little apartment overlooking a white beach and sheltered cove where I anchored *Dove* and buttoned her up.

My mother flew out from California and stayed with us for three weeks. She and Patti eyed each other a bit cautiously at first but they soon relaxed and enjoyed sharing kitchen chores and shopping. Then Ken MacLeish, son of the poet Archibald MacLeish, flew in from Washington and helped me write up the second part of my three-part series for *National Geographic*. Like the first article, it was the journal's cover story, and it brought in, so they told me, a bigger reader response than any other feature in the magazine's long history. Truthfully I could have done without the publicity, because people on harbor walls and in the yacht clubs recognized me or the name of the boat, and I was always being cornered and asked questions on my voyage.

Most people were nice but there were always name-dropping types around. These pestered me just because I was in the news. One invited us to dinner and when we were seated told us with a smug grin that he'd bet a friend he'd get us to his home. He won his bet but not our friendship. We soon got wise to these types.

We spent a dreamy month in Barbados, water skiing, skin diving, riding horses along the beach. What I enjoyed most were hot water showers and sleeping in a home that held still. After restless catnaps at sea I began to learn what real sleep was like again. My mind unwound because I wasn't always listening for a change of wind or wave pattern. We toured the island on a motorcycle. There was one spot on a grass hill that we really loved. We took picnics up there and lay around under trees that had been bent by the trade winds. It was all so relaxing and good.

When my nerves no longer felt sandpapered, we flew out to Fort Lauderdale to look for a boat in which to complete the last part of my journey around the world. I had some pretty fixed ideas in my mind about the boat. She had to be more than thirty feet long so that she could take any storm, and she had to have enough headroom below so that I could stand up without cracking my skull. She had to be of fiberglass because a wood boat would require too much maintenance, and she would have to have a diesel engine. The advantage of diesel is that it is less expensive and less explosive than gasoline.

I eventually found just the boat I was looking for in the Catskills yard of the Allied Boat Company in New York. They gave us a good discount, and with the advance royalties from my magazine articles we found we could afford her. Shivering in the winter cold, Patti and I watched the new boat being completed in the shipyard. She was a beautifully designed thirty-three-foot fiberglass sloop. I added extra equipment to help me sail her alone, and most importantly a self-steering vane.

The self-steering device which my father and I had designed for little Dove had worked well; but the Hassler gear selected for the new boat was more refined—the same type of rig Sir Francis Chichester had used to make his lone circumnavigation. We named the steering vane Gandalf, for the wizard in the Tolkien books.

To the new boat's basic layout I added extra storage, a chain plate, a rig for a staysail and roller-furling gear for two headsails.

The Hudson River was still iced up, so we trucked the new boat down to Fort Lauderdale, where we installed a depth-sounder, took aboard spare parts for most emergencies and stocked up with provisions. Then we invited Patti's father, Allen Ratterree, and her stepmother, Ann, to join us for a short shakedown cruise to the Bahamas.

Patti launched the new boat with a bottle of California champagne and named her the *Return of Dove*, but whenever we referred to the two boats we always spoke of *Little Dove* and *Big Dove*.

There followed wonderful days, then weeks, then months as Patti and I cruised the Bahamas and later the Virgin Islands. In the Fijis, where Patti and I had first met, we had believed we could not again discover such happiness. But in South Africa we had been even happier; and now in the Caribbean we were to discover that happiness has no frontiers, that it's a state of mind and not a possession, not a set route through life, not a goal to be gained but something that steals in gently like an evening mist or the morning sunlight—something beyond our control.

Our mood might best be understood by quoting directly from the tapes we made as we discovered new islands and unpeopled beaches, or when simply resting through sun-washed hours and starlit nights. Our electronic diary is a running commentary on two young people in love. Here, then, are some more excerpts from our tape recordings:

MARCH 21 [1968]: *We anchored Big Dove beside the little lighthouse outside Cat Cays harbor in the Bahamas and immediately went diving for crayfish. Speared five in no time at all. The trimaran Tahata came over and the couple aboard, Leo and Joy, didn't know how to spear fish. I showed Leo some pointers, but you can't learn to spear fish overnight, so we gave them our lobsters.*

MARCH 24: *Got a whole bunch of lobsters this morning and Patti made a stuffed lobster dinner. I told her I'd only married her for her cooking so she threatened a galley strike. We shared our* dinner with two new friends from the yacht Kaelu. In the afternoon I speared a big moray. It wiggled off the spear and chased me. My pulse went up to about 200. But I learned not to attack monsters in their own environment.

MARCH 25: Arrived at Bimini and immediately went diving. It's an absolutely new world down there under the surface. I was sort of cruising around looking at the fantastic colors when I found myself facing a lot of teeth. It was one of those ordinary sharks you see in an aquarium. While the shark was deciding which of my legs he was going to have for breakfast I leaped onto a rock ledge and yelled to Patti to rescue me in the dinghy. How we laughed. Boy! I still get nervous when sharks are around.

APRIL 13: Glorious sail to Nassau. Big Dove is a dream. She loves light airs and when the wind is up she moves at six to seven knots where Little Dove would sail at only four or five. Saw two whales mating right in front of our bow. Patti saw them first. I released the wind vane and changed course. You don't argue with whales at any time. I know of four cases of boats being charged by whales. Patti was so fascinated that she didn't understand the danger. I told her how world-circling sailor Alan Eddy had had a hairy time in the Indian Ocean when his thirty-foot yacht Apogee ran over a sleeping whale. Alan told me how his boat was immediately attacked by twenty whales. They struck low down in the way they would hit a shark in the liver. The fact that the Apogee survived with minor damage gave me more confidence in Dove because she was made by the same company. Anyway, Patti and I just sailed right past the colossal lovers who just lay there spouting and having a good time.

APRIL 20: Glad to be out of Nassau. It's an awful place, everything so expensive and full of tourist traps. Even parrot fish sell in Nassau for two dollars and more a pound, and conchs, which we eat when we've got nothing else, sell for twenty-five cents each. Conchs are as common as coconuts—and it hurts to pay for coconuts.

APRIL 22: Last night was so balmy that we decided to sleep in the cockpit. About two o'clock we were awakened by a weird sound. We had anchored in a narrow cay. Slipping past us was a 150-foot boat with no lights. Suddenly a searchlight swept across the water. The boat stayed there for fifteen minutes. Then it reversed out of the cay and disappeared. The whole scene was like something out of a mystery thriller. Everyone knows there are smugglers here and I'll bet this was a smuggler's boat. I wonder how safe we'd have been if they'd known we had watched the operation. One of our friends warned us not to know too much. Weird things are going on all the time. One guy found a beer crate and broke open a bottle. It was filled with hundred-dollar bills. Paradise Island is said to be liked by the Mafia. Okay, let them have it. We'll find our own.

APRIL 23: Sailed to an unoccupied island and found a citrus grove with oranges rotting on the ground. We helped ourselves. The fruit is very bitter but it makes a terrific drink.

APRIL 26: Arrived Spanish Wells. Many of the islanders have the same name and are fanatically religious. I tried to buy some beer and they looked at me as if I were the devil's sidekick. As Patti and I walked down a street of small stores we felt a hundred eyes watching us. We had the feeling we were going to be stoned any time, medieval fashion. I kidded Patti that she was going to be burned as a witch and offered to buy her a broomstick. We were glad to be back on Dove. Been trying out Gandalf [the wind vane] and it's working well. Dove now scooting at six knots in an eighteen-knot wind, and we're trailing a dinghy. Patti's in the dinghy, not for punishment but because she's trying to take photographs. She's holding on like fun as the dinghy planes over the water. At any minute I'm going to have to rescue her.

APRIL 29: Arrived at Rose island. Went diving and speared a grouper for breakfast. As I was trying to get the fish aboard a shark circled and gave me the once-over.

Patti made some salt water bread. It's really good. Here's her recipe.

One tablespoon of dried yeast, one tablespoon of sugar, four cups of flour, one and a half cups of seawater. Dissolve the yeast and sugar in the salt water, then mix in the flour. Put the mixture into a well-greased pan. Let it stand for two hours to rise. Cook covered on low flame for half an hour on each side in a heavy pan. Eat when hot.

Now we'll have bread all the way to Saint Thomas in the Virgins.

Been teaching other yachtsmen around here how to navigate. I'm always amazed how little some people know about sailing. A lot of inexperienced people go cruising before they know what they're getting into.

APRIL 30: Patti had a bad pain in her stomach. I remembered when my appendix started to explode in Polynesia, and I dashed around trying to find a doctor. Eventually found a nurse who says Patti's okay. I've been teaching Leo and Joy and Bill and the others how to navigate, and Patti too. She's getting quite good. Just collected another cat and called him Gollum [another Hobbit character]. It's a strange creature which likes its comforts.

Patti sometimes kept up our tape recorder diary. On May 20 Patti recorded:

This is me, Patti, speaking. Robin is up the mast trying to mend a broken halyard. For the past ten days we've been sailing through wretched weather to the Virgins. The Tahata, which sailed out with us from Spanish Wells, was demasted and Dove is really taking a pounding. When one squall hit us Robin thought the wind reached sixty knots. I was really scared especially when the genny halyard broke. I've just hoisted Robin up the mast in the bosun's chair. The first time he went up the mast without my help. I was in the cabin. I called to him and when he didn't answer I came up on deck. No sign of Robin. Honestly I thought I was going to die of fright. I figured that he could only have fallen overboard and here I was sailing along in Dove at quite a good speed. I was just wondering if I could turn the boat around by myself when I heard Robin shouting down from the spreaders, and asking what was the matter. I told him if he gave me a fright like that again I'd throw him to the sharks.

Anyway, I'm beginning to understand what Robin has been through when he sails alone. We've got tons of canned food aboard but it all seems so blah. You look at a can and it just looks like a can. How we long for fresh food again. Robin can work up some enthusiasm when he opens a can of oysters. Not me! Canned oysters in a rough sea—aagh!

It's good for us to know bad weather and rough sailing. It makes us appreciate the good days when the sea looks so marvelous that you want to drink it. I mean, life would be pretty monotonous if the sky was always blue. That sounds like a cliche, so how else shall I put it? I think both of us are suspicious of having life too easy. You know, everything too pretty. We've talked over our future sometimes, and it's pretty vague, but neither of us wants to spend the rest of our lives in Polynesian fashion—endless days of eating and swimming and parties and laughing. Both of us want to know the seasons—winters as well as springs and summers. I understand why Robin enjoys a storm. He likes the risk and danger.

It's now slashing with rain. The raindrops are coming in at us like angled needles. We've collected a lot of fresh water off the sails and in the upturned dinghy. A gal's got to have a bath sometime, and it looks as if mine's coming up pretty soon.

My next entry on the tape was May 16, 1969. I recorded:

We've just sighted Saint Thomas in the Virgins. This is our sixteenth day at sea, and it's sure been a long and tiring trip, in fact one of the worst I've ever had. Patti was a bit seasick but she's better now. The cats are having a ball, though Kili is usually scared of bad weather. Fili doesn't seem to mind the weather either way. Gollum loves the storms. He comes out on the deck when it's raining, sticks his nose in the air and sniffs the wind. I hope we're going to have fun in the Virgins. Patti deserves some fun for the way she's taken this stormy trip. See you later. . . .

We did not make another tape for several weeks, because when we reached the Virgins I flew off at once to Barbados to sail *Little*

Dove back to Saint Thomas. It was weird sailing the little boat again. She seemed like a toy after *Big Dove*, and I couldn't imagine how I had managed to sail her most of the way around the world. The distance from Barbados to the Virgins is about five hundred sea miles and as I'd not brought along my sextant, I had to rely on dead reckoning for navigation. The danger was getting too close to shore. When I was off Montserrat the wind died altogether and I fell asleep at the tiller. When I awoke the wind had picked up and I found I was sailing directly for a reef half a mile ahead. Another few minutes of sleep and *Little Dove* would have had it—and me too probably.

I brought *Little Dove* into Saint Thomas on the evening of June 11—two days earlier than I had expected. Patti was busy sewing in the cabin when I jumped aboard. I pushed open the companionway door, and found myself looking right into a pistol. There was a finger on the trigger.

"Don't you ever scare me like that again," said Patti as she lowered the gun.

Patti had had reason to be scared. In the previous months there had been a number of muggings and rapes in this area. She had not been expecting me for at least another day so when she heard someone jump aboard she was sure it was one of the muggers. Patti's aim looked pretty good to me so I was glad she didn't shoot at sight.

We spent a month cleaning up *Little Dove*, stripping off the Atlantic barnacles and then repainting her. With her brightwork polished and her hull and decks glistening once more, she looked prettier than she'd ever been. We tied a red "For Sale" sign to the poop deck rail. I felt like Judas. Here was this little boat which had carried me so far through hell, high water and sometimes close to heaven, and now I was selling her for pieces of silver—or greenbacks, I hoped.

We left *Little Dove* in Saint Thomas and sailed *Big Dove* out to explore the Virgins. Here are some more quotes from the tapes:

AUGUST 6: *We've decided to stay out in the Virgins until the* hurricane season is over. In Puerto Rico they have a superstition that if the avocado crop doesn't do well it will be a bad year for hurricanes. They have had a really bad avocado crop. I don't go much for superstition—but just in case they're right we plan to hole up here anyway. Actually there was a warning a week ago, and we scooted into Hurricane Hole off Saint John's, Big Dove towing Little Dove into good anchorage. I put out all the ground tackle we had, but fortunately Hurricane Anna missed the Virgins and we were okay.

We managed to sell Little Dove for $4,725. I wonder how she will like her new owner. Just hope he's good to her. Patti and I sailed Big Dove round Little Dove in a last salute. We were really sad, and so we went over to a small hotel and listened to a Calypso singer.

AUGUST 20: Arrived Leinster Bay and went diving. We dove among the reefs and then Patti got her first lobster and a fish with her new spear gun. I bought her the spear gun because she can't use the hand sling. The hand sling is too hard for her to pull back. Patti absurdly pleased with her shooting, of course, and she claimed the fish tasted much better than anything I'd caught. Two sharks are now snooping around the boat, but they don't bother us too much. In the evenings we read aloud to each other. We're very happy.

AUGUST 22: Radio warning about Hurricane Donna coming our way, so we decided to get closer to Hurricane Hole, which is pretty well protected. We eventually pulled into Dead Man's Bay, arriving just at dark. Whole bay is filled with craft waiting for the storm. I powered around looking for a place to anchor. Most of the places were about forty feet deep and that would mean putting out too much chain. Not many boats carry heavy chain, but I believe in putting money into anchor gear instead of into insurance. I find it close to impossible without an anchor winch to pull up three-eighths-inch chain when it's forty feet deep. So we anchored in the lee of the point and it was really nice. Storm failed to arrive so we went diving next morning. A huge shark moved up on me with all its teeth showing. It wasn't after me at all but chasing some silver fish about a foot long in a feeding frenzy. Anyway, I wasn't going to wait around and see if that brute wanted a change of diet.

AUGUST 24: Some people here at a place called The Bitter End in Gorda Sound are building a resort. They have found a really lovely spot and they've hauled in all the material they need. Basil Symonette, one of the resort owners, asked me to help them build the place, so I've decided to do that and earn some money while waiting out the hurricane season. . . .

Our taped record stopped for a while because for the next few months I became a landlubber, helping to build the resort at The Bitter End. Just as in Darwin, I found I was quite useful with my hands, and was able to put in walls, windows, tile bathrooms and that sort of thing. Dove was anchored out in the bay, and when Patti's household chores were done she would join me. She was useful with a paintbrush and she planted a garden. There were no union rules, so when we felt like it we took time off and went fishing or cruised about. I took my work seriously not only because it paid well but because I saw it as experience for the time when I planned to build a home of our own. We would know just how to build our home when the time arrived.

With the hurricane season over, I made plans to sail the thousand miles to Panama. We found a ship, the Lurline, sailing for the Canal on November 20 and after getting Patti aboard and arranging to meet her in Porvenir, one of the San Blas islands, I put to sea again.

Fili and Kili were my only passengers because Gollum had found another owner. When Gollum was missing a few days before we were due to sail, we made inquiries and learned that he had been seen in the house of a millionaire—one of those beautiful, white-walled cliffside places with soft-footed servants and fountained swimming pools—the whole works. Gollum was probably curled up on a tasseled cushion and had no intention of returning to the discomforts of life at sea.

In the Virgins I had installed a freezer which ran off the engine and while I watched the *Lurline* sail west I made my first iced drink and then told the tape recorder:

Saint Croix now on my beam and I'm making about six knots. At this speed the gunwales of Little Dove would be awash. . . . I'm really confident about this leg of the voyage. Big Dove's a good boat and it's exciting to be sailing once again.

In the late afternoon a small plane swooped low over *Dove* and the *National Geographic* man aboard presumably took pictures. Then a heavy rain squall hit and I stood naked on the deck to take a bath. All seemed well until I lit the stove to cook an enchilada TV supper. There must have been a kerosene leak because the flare-up singed my eyelashes. Soot was all over the cabin and there was no Patti to clean it up. A bachelor's life, I decided, was not for me.

I opened up the ports to get fresh air and was immediately hit by another squall. The genoa had become snarled up, and in the time that it took me to untangle it the cabin was soaked. I'd obviously been too long on land.

Fire and water—what next? I asked the tape, and had hardly put the question when I saw a ship on collision course. I pulled over the tiller, threw some four-letter words across the water and took some comfort in the idea that troubles only come in threes. But not for me. Next day Gandalf broke—the wooden oarlike blade that goes into the water. That would mean a delay at the Canal, for I hate to steer myself and I had no intention of doing so in the long Pacific haul to California.

Big Dove had a useful inboard engine so when the wind dropped I was able to power at four or five knots. By the time I reached the San Blas islands I had used up all my fuel. I anchored *Dove* off a beach at Porvenir just eight days after leaving Saint Thomas. My taffrail log recorded 1,099 miles. The straight-line distance from Saint Thomas was 139 miles shorter, but you can't always sail in a straight line. I rowed ashore and looked for Patti. The only hotel seemed the obvious place and I was just climbing the front porch when out she came—flying.

Patti had arrived only a few hours before, because the S.S. *Lurline* had called at other ports along the route to Panama. She had flown from Panama in a private plane. She had had a wretched sea voyage and had been sick every morning. She had consulted the ship's doctor and we were still embracing on the hotel steps when Patti told me the medical diagnosis.

"Guess what. Robin—it looks like you might be a father."

The right thing for me to have done was to have shouted hallelujahs, to have handed out cigars and dashed off to buy a diamond clasp or something. Actually her news felt like a kick in the guts. I was suddenly sick with fear for her. Sure I'd had my biology and hygiene classes at school, but what I thought of was my mother's story of my own birth.

I had been a Caesarean baby, and when I was quite young my mother had told me how she had nearly died in giving me life. She could hardly have guessed the effect this disclosure would have had on her small son. I was left with a horror of childbirth.

Patti completely misunderstood my alarm. She pushed me away and studied me, her eyes troubled.

"Oh, Robin, I thought you'd be so thrilled with the news. When we talked about having children you always seemed so excited. Oh, honey, I just don't understand you."

"No," I said, "it's not that at all. It's hard to explain. I just . . ."

"You don't want the baby, do you?" insisted Patti. "Let's at least be honest." Tears welled up into her eyes. "Anyway, I don't know for sure yet."

Above our heads the wind was swinging a bar sign in about three languages. The sign wheezed like an old man with asthma. I just didn't know what to say. Thoughts tumbled around my mind. One part of me was jolted by the idea that I could create life— not an unpleasant one at all. But the other thought was that Patti was going to pay a horrible price in pain and sickness. Perhaps she would die, I thought.

How wrong I was! Throughout her pregnancy Patti glowed with health. Her skin took on a fresh childlike bloom and there was a sort of peace about her I hadn't recognized before. My fear for her simply melted away. She didn't have to lecture me or anything or tell me I was just being a fool. I began to see that the baby was part of our lives, part of our love.

We spent two months exploring the Panama islands, sometimes staying on *Dove*, more often in the homes of new friends. The few Cuna Indians who had not come in contact with the tourists were helpful, artistic and friendly. On the tourist tracks, though, we found them infected by the discourtesy and greed of the western world.

Patti had picked up quite a lot of Spanish and was able to bargain successfully for provisions and souvenirs. At Tigre island, just off the mainland, we found whole families of albinos, descendants of the ones the Spaniards had found centuries before, who had given rise to the report that a lost white tribe had settled in the San Blas islands.

Among our new white friends were Tom and Joan Moody, who had sold their business in the United States and built a fascinating resort at Pidertupo. Wisely they had patterned their cottages on the local architecture. They had built a small airstrip on an adjacent island so that tourists could fly in and "go native" a few hours after leaving the concrete jungles to the north.

I sailed *Dove* to Cristobal in the Canal Zone and there we spent Christmas in an American home. A candlelit tree, carols sung round a piano and the exchange of presents recalled the happiest moments of my boyhood.

On New Year's Day Patti and I decided to return some of the hospitality we'd received and invited about thirty people to a Hawaiian luau with Polynesian overtones. What our planned party amounted to was a pig feast on the beach, but first we had to find the pig. We went to a small farmhouse in the country, knocked on the door and an enormous black man appeared. He was dressed in full armor like a conquistador. The armor had been beaten out of tin cans, but his sword was real enough and when he drew it from its sheath we beat a fast retreat. Eventually we found a pig of the right size and built an *umu* (underground oven) in the sand, then pushed the pig between hot rocks to roast. Without a luau recipe book we had to guess the roasting period. Our guesswork was about an hour out, and the pig was so well cooked its head fell off.

We learned. too, never to roast a pig in sand. The noise of about six hundred teeth, real and false, crunching sandy pork was like a heavy truck on a newly graveled driveway. The guests were marvelously polite and assured us that there was no sand at all—in the beer.

Unrelated to this experience was a long session for me at the local dentist. For eighty dollars the dentist extracted two aching molars and filled ten cavities. The surgery was good but one of my gums would not stop bleeding. Back at the yacht club I was being offered Kleenex and sympathy when I suddenly keeled over and passed out. When I came around there were half a dozen uniformed firemen fussing over me.

When I'd fainted a fireman at the next table had caught me and instead of getting a doctor he had summoned the local fire brigade. Presumably because they were short on first aid drill, the firemen forced an oxygen mask over my face. Whether it was the oxygen or a couple of shots of brandy that put me on my feet again was a question noisily debated by the retreating brigade. The upshot was that within the hour I was able to take Patti to a James Bond film. We quite enjoyed it too.

Actually, before we left for the movie a doctor arrived to check me over. By strange coincidence this was the doctor who had flown Patti from Panama to the San Blas islands. He had given Patti a pregnancy test but it had proved negative. But Patti had gone back for a second test two weeks later and had bet the doctor a dollar that she wasn't going to have a baby. When the doctor saw Patti at the yacht club he wrote out a note, folded it over and handed it to her with a grin. We read it as we drove in a taxi to the theater. The note read "You owe me a dollar!"

Spare parts for *Dove's* broken wind vane arrived from England in mid-January and I was at last ready to sail through the Canal.

One question to be decided was where to go when *Dove* had reached the Pacific. I looked forward to journey's end because I'd been at sea (more or less) for nearly a quarter of my life. But now there was another factor which decided our immediate future.

"What about the baby?" I asked Patti as I signed up the documents to get us through the Canal. "Shouldn't it be born in California? I mean, you'll need the best medical care, a hospital and all that."

"Women have babies in treetops and probably at the North Pole," she said. "Anyway, I bet he'll whistle sea chanteys before he talks."

"He?" I said.

"Fifty-fifty chance." She laughed. "If it's a girl she'll be a tomboy for sure."

Her eyes were far away when she added, "I wonder if there's any truth in the theory that a child is prenatally influenced by its mother's environment. I remember reading somewhere about a pregnant woman spending all her time in art galleries and listening to Beethoven. The child turned out masterpieces and played piano concertos before he was ten."

"You believe that?" I asked.

"I'd like to. And if it's true what would you like your child to be? Disc jockey, president or candlestick maker? I could probably fix it. Supposing I looked at the stars all night—do you think he'd be the first man to walk on Jupiter?"

I bent over the top of the chair and kissed her forehead. She looked like a blond madonna. "I'd want him to love nature. I'd want him to love animals, mountains, clean water, sea life. I'd want him to understand all these things," I said.

"That's easy. Let's go to the Galápagos islands," said Patti lightly.

This wasn't the only reason why we decided on the Galápagos before turning north for the run to California. Patti had been there five years earlier and had absolutely loved the islands. She knew that I would love them too.

Getting through the Panama Canal in a small boat is not all that simple. When the water level changes in the locks it becomes very turbulent and there is a real risk of crushing a hull or losing a mast. The law forbids you to sail your own boat through the Canal and I was forced to hand over *Dove* to a pilot and four linesmen. So long as I did not interfere with the navigation, the Canal Company would be responsible for any damage, but it was not easy to keep my hands off the tiller when *Dove* rolled about in the swirl of water in the Gatún Locks and was threatened by other ships.

With barely a hull scratch we reached Balboa, on the Pacific side, on January 17. Before I sailed for the Galápagos, Patti and I spent a terrific ten days together anchored off Taboga island, a two-hour sail from the Canal. On Taboga we mostly lay around in the sun and read. One thing the long voyage had done for me was to give me a pretty wide taste in literature. I had gone through quite a library in five years and been introduced to authors ranging from Robert Louis Stevenson to Ruark, from Hemingway to Agatha Christie. If I ever returned to school I would have a lot of catching up to do in the math class, but at least I'd have a head start in English literature and geography.

We returned to Balboa to drop off Patti and to arrange for her to travel to the Galápagos islands by steamer and by plane.

"And don't forget," I said, as I boarded *Dove* on January 30, "to bring along my son."

"No problem," Patti laughed. "He's still very attached to me."

~~ 10

Creatures That Hath Life

DARWIN HAD BEEN only six years older than I now was when he first set foot in the Galápagos. But he was a scientist and I was a sailor. I'd been reading his journal while I was on the eleven-hundred-mile, eight-day sail from Panama to San Cristóbal. My voyage was almost trouble-free except when I nearly knocked myself out on the tiller.

It sounds a bit heavy, but I liked one phrase Darwin used about the Galápagos. He said: "Here we seem to be brought to that great fact of history—that mystery of mysteries—the first appearance of a new being on this earth."

In the Galápagos I often thought I was pretty close to the "mystery of mysteries."

The depth-sounder helped me feel my way into Wreck Harbor on an inky night and next morning I went ashore to check up on news of Patti. There was none and the next mail wasn't due for several days. I was sour and a bit worried. I hadn't a clue where she was.

The cats wanted some attention. Blind Fili was pregnant. She had picked up some infection, but a few shots of an antibiotic provided by a doctor in Ecuador put her on her feet again, and she later gave birth to two live kittens—Pooh and Piglet. I knew the kittens' father because I'd caught Fili with a midnight-cowboy sort of cat on the Atlantic side of the Canal. At the time I had thought it was a pretty lousy thing to take advantage of a blind lady who'd gotten lost on her way home. Anyway, the kittens were cute.

A cable arrived from Patti to say she would be flying out from Guayaquil in Ecuador the following day. The only airport in the Galápagos was on Baltra island, fifty miles away, so I ran all the way back to Dove and sailed under full canvas. I was just in time to see the plane touch down, but Patti wasn't among the passengers. I discovered later that although she had had her reservation she had lost her place to Ecuadorian servicemen, who always have priority. She sent a message to me by another passenger to say she would be on the next plane, two days later. Two days is a long time to hang around an airport.

When the next plane arrived Patti disembarked with her father and stepmother. For the next ten days the four of us explored the islands. The Ratterrees were great company. Right from the start there was a fifth member of the party—the ghost of Charles Darwin, who breathed down our necks.

We saw Darwin's "finches that shook the world." Darwin had listed thirteen different types of finches and they helped him build up his theory which challenged the age-old belief that the world was created in six days.

The most fascinating finch is the Santa Cruz woodpecker, which uses a twig or cactus spine as a tool to burrow into trees for grubs. This bird uses twigs as easily as a carpenter uses a screwdriver.

On reaching Plaza island we had a marvelous time playing around with sea lions. They were more like puppies in the way they picked up sticks and brought them back to us.

Patti was no longer bikini-trim, but she almost held her own in an underwater tug of war with a young sea lion that never tired of playing. When we had enough of the game the sea lions sulked and then began to catch the waves and surf to the shore in a style that would have won the Malibu beach title.

Because it comes in on the Humboldt Current, the water around the Galápagos is quite cold. We found we could not swim for long. Like the marine iguanas we sought out rocks, which reach a temperature of 120 degrees in the noonday sun. When I discarded my shorts in a secluded cove I discovered how hot the sun can be in these tropical islands. That night I couldn't sit down.

Most evenings our dinner menu was fresh fish or lobster which I'd caught or speared an hour or two earlier. No one has really eaten lobster until he has tried the Galápagos variety. I discovered my first one by accident when looking for groupers in a pool off James Bay. Patti and I had speared so many groupers that day that there was no more freezer room to store them, but I went on diving because I could not tear myself away from the fascinating colors and lava formations beneath the surface. Then on the edge of a shelf I spotted an extraordinary prehistoric creature.

Back on *Dove's* deck I taped: *Went looking for starfish species when I saw something strange lying in a foot of water. It looked like a crayfish but there was something very weird about it. Instead of antennae up front it had flippers like a sand crab's and its shell was quite different. I touched it cautiously and then grabbed it and threw it in the dinghy. I thought: Well, if there's one of these there might be a relative close by. Sure enough I found number two. The third one was suspicious of me and almost escaped, but within ten minutes I had caught five of these weird creatures. . . . Patti barbecued them (they're really hard to open) and we've just eaten them for dinner. If one of those Hollywood restaurateurs gets to hear about the Galápagos lobsters they'll be breeding them in basement aquariums.*

With such discoveries I often felt I was looking at evolutionary potter's clay. The "gentle dragons"—the marine iguanas—seemed to waddle right out of the mists of time. No wonder the Spaniards called this corner of the world Las Islas Encantadas ("The Enchanted Isles"). The thirteen islands of the archipelago (five are volcanic) have created the world's best natural history laboratory. Fortunately Ecuador has recently declared the islands a protected reserve and has given the wildlife legal defense against the worst of predators—man.

Galápagos was first ravaged a long time ago when English pirates used the islands as a base for attacking the treasure-laden ships of Spain. These pirate ships probably brought the rats which have wiped out much of the wildlife. Baltra island was occupied by the United States in World War II and the land iguanas were used as pistol targets by bored servicemen. Only a handful of the land iguanas survived the Baltra massacre.

For more than a century whaling ships and merchantmen have stopped at the Galápagos to take on provisions, and too many captains' logbooks speak of taking huge numbers of land tortoises. Typically, Captain David Porter, who commanded the U.S. Navy frigate *Essex*, recorded in 1815: "Here to be obtained are land tortoises in great numbers. They are highly esteemed for their excellence and weigh three to four hundredweight each. Vessels . . . generally take aboard two to three hundred of these animals and stow them in the holds where, strange as it may appear, they have been known to live for a year without food or water."

One estimate is that 400,000 have been slaughtered or seized in the past century and there are now not 10,000 left. I get angry when I find statistics like these and I just hope that enough of my generation get as stirred up as I do to prevent the world being stripped before it becomes as dead as the moon.

While we Americans self-righteously point our fingers at Japanese whalers scouring the oceans for the last of the whales, we like to forget what we did to the great herds of buffalo! As we explored the Galápagos my anger mounted against all who ravage our planet.

With the islands' weird currents and with rocks just below the surface, sailing around the Galápagos can be tricky, so we decided to leave *Dove* for a few days in Academy Bay at Santa Cruz and sail in a local powered boat, the *Vagabond*, chartered by *National*

Geographic. The advantage of the charter boat was that it allowed me to relax for a bit and not worry about the chores of sailing Dove. I had more time to appreciate this strange and magic world. On the tape recorder I reported our day-by-day adventures:

FEBRUARY 26: Went ashore on little Hood island, the southernmost of the group, and was fascinated by the mockingbirds, which crave fresh water. If you hold a teaspoonful in your hand they fly down and suck up the drops. The booby birds were just as tame.

Climbed lava rocks and came across a colony of marine iguanas, incredibly colored in reds and greens. It's their mating season and they have put on all their war paint to go courting. . . . Discovered a blowhole in the cliffs where the surf sweeping in from the Pacific is thrown up thirty feet. A baby fur seal nuzzled up to Patti and nibbled at her fingers.

FEBRUARY 28: Back on Dove. I powered to James Bay on San Salvador island. We were pretty pooped after a tiring trip, but we went ashore to watch the turtles laying eggs. Bob Madden [a National Geographic photographer] tried to get up close but one turtle did not like him and kicked sand into his eyes. Bob had red eyes for quite a while and I'll bet there's a moral here somewhere.

MARCH 1: Went ashore looking for pigs. The pirates or early settlers brought in the first pigs and goats, which have gone quite wild and now threaten the indigenous wildlife. I borrowed an antique rifle and managed to shoot two goats. The herds of goats have to be thinned out, and the shooting sure helps to keep down our meat bills.

MARCH 2: A local man has been telling me of a salt mine near here where ten miners live off the land. It seems that they each ate ten doves a day for ten months. Total cost 30,000 birds. Walked for half a mile to a beautiful pool where seals were diving around and playing. Sailed to Buccaneer Cave, named for seventeenth-century pirates who hung out here. It's weird and you can easily imagine pirates with wooden legs and patches over their eyes walking among the dark lava rocks.

MARCH 3: Ashore and had a terrific dinner (Al Ratterree the

cook) of wild goat ribs and then powered back to Baltra island to see Al and Ann off by plane.

MARCH 4: Returned to Academy Bay to haul out Dove. This turned out to be an interesting operation. I tied Dove to a pier, and when the tide went out she was left almost high and dry. I was cleaning off the barnacles and standing in a foot of water when a puffer fish sneaked up and bit my toe. Oh! the hazards of the sea!

MARCH 5: My birthday, so Patti baked a cake. The boat was tilted over so the cake was shaped like a door wedge, but it tasted a lot better than it looked. Painting a boat is an awful way to spend a twenty-first birthday!

MARCH 6: All the populated islands have a seacoast town and an inland town. In the seacoast towns the people live off fishing and tourists and in the inland towns they are farmers. Took a day off from cleaning up Dove and went up to a farming town and then trekked to the rim of a dead volcano. Got pretty thirsty but the island's water is hard to drink. It's brackish and awful, but the islanders don't seem to mind. In fact, when they drink fresh rainwater they put salt in it to make it "nice."

MARCH 7: Last night Bob Madden tried to take pictures of a yellow warbler nest and climbed a poisonous tree. His neck looks as if it's been badly burned. Found a doctor, whose injection helped.

Patti and I sailed alone around the tip of Isabela island for Fernandina island. There was no one around so we took our clothes off. It was very funny the way some porpoises swam over and sort of tilted their heads sideways to take a closer look. They'd probably never seen any naked human before. Patti got most of the looks, perhaps because she is five months pregnant. It's the tameness of the wildlife that's so fascinating. The animals don't seem to have any fear of us. They sort of accept us.

MARCH 13: We're sailing under the volcanic mountain on Isabela's northern shore. It's towering 5,600 feet above us—desolate but beautiful. The lava has trickled down in huge trails to the ocean, and at the mountain's crest there's a little crown of clouds. If I hadn't seen this mountain I couldn't have even dreamed it up. . . . Around the next cove and the cliffs are rising hundreds of feet and are streaked bright red as if the rocks are bleeding. The view here is really amazing. . . . Evening now and we've just anchored Dove beyond the surf. . . . It's dark now and quite hairy listening to the huge waves pounding against the cliff face.

MARCH 14: Arrived Fernandina—a cruel-looking island with lava rocks streaking down to a shore lined with mangrove trees. Small fiords full of fish cut into the land like slices taken from cake. One lagoon is filled with flightless cormorants. Their wings look like tattered laundry. They waddle up the rocks using their wings to keep their balance. I rowed the dinghy through twisted channels to a small lava hill like a little world on its own. Brilliantly red-colored crabs scuttle over the dark lava rocks. They are called Sally Lightfoots. The sun is right over our heads at the equinox, but the water here is still cool and really refreshing. As we lay on the rocks some penguins waddled over to take a look at us. The penguins came in on the cold Peru current.

MARCH 15: Oh, God, is it true that there are cities somewhere and that people live in concrete egg boxes!

Patti and I are alone now in a wonderland which you can't really describe. This morning I threw fish scraps over the side and some pelicans flew in to clean them up. One bird had a bad tear in its pouch, and we watched it trying to scoop up food. Everything it took into its bill just floated out again. We saw that it would soon die of starvation. I jumped over the side of Dove and grabbed it while Patti took some pictures. We brought the pelican aboard— it was covered with black bugs. Patti broke open the first-aid equipment. The wound needed about twenty nylon stitches. Then I drilled two holes and wired up the broken bill with stainless steel. The operation took me an hour. Then I threw the pelican back overboard.

MARCH 16: The pelican I fixed up yesterday is back again. We've been watching him hold all the fish we throw him. In fact he can outdo all the others in picking up the scraps. It's great! Fernandina island is the most exciting of them all. The underwater life and colors are fantastic. It's the most marvelous diving I've done anywhere. When we're tired of swimming around we go ashore and lie naked on the hot rocks, along with a bunch of iguanas, who take us for granted. We feel like we're part of where it all began— I mean, part of creation and life. . . .

I didn't record it on the tape, but something quite odd happened here. When I'd been in New Guinea I'd bought a Bible. I don't know what made me do it except I just had a vague idea that I'd like to read the Bible sometime. I bought a Koran too. In case anyone might think me religious or something I had wrapped the Bible in the lurid jacket of a detective story. I never did get around to reading the Bible—at least not until that evening when we were anchored off Fernandina.

I was waiting for dinner—Patti was cooking some lobster and I was wondering how to fill out the time. On sudden impulse I took the Bible from the shelf and went up on deck. Page one seemed to be the best place to start. When you read the first chapter of Genesis in the light of a stained-glass window it may mean one thing. When you read it by the light of a Galápagos sunset, it surely means another. Prehistoric turtles were swimming around the boat and pelicans were flying above as I read:

And God said, Let the waters bring forth abundantly the moving creature that hath life, and fowl that may fly above the earth in the open firmament of heaven.

And God created great whales, and every living creature that moveth, which the waters brought forth abundantly, after their kind, and every winged fowl after his kind; and God saw that it was good.

And God blessed them, saying, Be fruitful, and multiply, and fill the waters in the seas, and let fowl multiply in the earth. . . .

Patti called me for dinner just as I had reached verse 26:

And God said, Let us make man in our image, after our likeness: and let them have dominion over the fish of the sea, and over the fowl of the air, and over the cattle, and over all the earth, and over every creeping thing that creepeth upon the earth.

So God created man in his own image, in the image of God created he him; male and female created he them.

And God blessed them, and God said unto them, Be fruitful, and multiply. . . .

I went down to the cabin. I patted Patti's swelling stomach and said, "And God saw that it was good."

Patti gave me a puzzled look. She thought I was talking about the lobsters and said, "What's got into you?" I produced the Bible from behind my back and told her, "Genesis sounds a lot better than anything old Darwin wrote."

Now Patti looked really surprised. "Okay, when we get back to California you can start your anti-Darwinian revolution." She scooped up some lobster flesh from the shell and added seriously, "I didn't know you read the Bible."

"There're a lot of things you don't know about me," I grinned.

The coffeepot began to boil over and we didn't continue the dialogue—not then.

We moved *Dove* from cove to cove, and there was always something unexpected turning up. For instance, I was diving around in a patch of blue water when a leopard ray glided into range of my spear gun. I don't know what the fish thought of me, but it was too beautiful to harm as it circled several times.

In the shallow water our movements disturbed the fine gray lava sand, and murky clouds would roll up and engulf me. I had the feeling of being out in space, weightless like an astronaut and sort of aware of infinity. In another place we spent hours swimming among mangrove roots which reached down into the water like an old man's fingers. Patti said they looked like an Impressionistic painting.

We ate when we were hungry and our meals were from a gourmet's cookbook—lobster, wild goat's meat, clams, baby octopus. We would sit cross-legged in the cockpit and eat off a table I'd slung from the boom.

Sometimes we backtracked Dove, but when we paid a return visit to a cove or beach it never looked as lovely the second time around. We'd find a lagoon that was really beautiful and return to it perhaps two days later, but the water was colder, the colors more subdued, the wildlife less interesting. After this had happened several times we learned not to look over our shoulders. It was the next place that mattered, the view around the next headland, the swim in the next lagoon.

Eventually the time arrived when we had to turn about. We sailed directly back to James Bay, where we found the inter-island fifty-passenger boat, called the Lina-A, anchored offshore. Lina-A was full of tourists, who came over to Dove and played twenty questions with us. It was awful. I found it hard to be patient with these people—especially the women with rasping voices and men with stomachs bulging over plaid Jamaica shorts. Some of these tourists think that they've explored the Galápagos when they've poked a stick at a turtle or chased an iguana up a rock.

Lina-A had an empty cabin and we fixed it up for Patti to sail to Baltra, from where she would fly to Ecuador and then sail back to California. We were so busy provisioning Dove on that last day together that there was hardly time to think about another separation—the last, I hoped.

Lina-A was due to sail at midnight and at eleven o'clock I rowed Patti across in the dinghy with all her gear. We had spent seven weeks in the Galápagos islands, two weeks longer than Darwin had done a century or more earlier. We were unlikely to come up with any new theories on how the world began, but we felt closer to that "mystery of mysteries—the first appearance of new beings upon this earth."

Patti was looking very pregnant but terrifically healthy, and as we strolled down the deck of Lina-A I mimicked her awkward walk, leaning back on my heels. We roared with laughter.

"You both look fine," I said, as I put a foot over the rail.

"Sure," said Patti. "Junior spends his time swimming around like his father. I just hope he's not born with webbed feet."

The crew of the *Lina-A* were preparing to raise the anchor. Patti covered my hands with her own.

"Honey, you're not afraid any more—I mean of the baby and me?"

"No. that's all gone," I said.

Bob Madden, the *National Geographic* staffman who had been with us in the Galápagos for a while, had told us how he and his wife had just had a baby by the natural method. His story had really excited us. He had told us what an easy time his wife had had and how he had been present at the birth and had actually helped her with breathing techniques and massage—that sort of thing. After we had listened to Bob tell the story of the birth of his child, Patti and I decided that that was the way we wanted our baby to be born. I think it was then that I really lost my fear of what Patti would have to go through.

I still had my leg dangling over the rail of the *Lina-A* when Patti said, "Now remember, Robin, we've made a pact. You've promised to be with me. No dilly-dallying on the way."

"Promise," I said.

"And our baby will start life as naturally as the baby porpoises," said Patti.

"And the iguanas."

"Yes, and the baby iguanas."

For a while we were silent, then Patti said, "Oh, it's so exciting, Robin—I mean the thought of you being with me, and I'm not going to have drugs or anything."

She squeezed my hands on the rail and a crewman passed and said, "Time for you to leave, sir."

I climbed down into the dinghy and then rowed around the *Lina-A*. The crazy thing was that I couldn't remember which side Patti's cabin was on. I peered up at the portholes but I didn't see her again—not for another thirty-eight days.

~ 11

Home Is the Sailor

FROM THE DECK of *Dove* I watched the lights of *Lina-A* fade and vanish, and then I snatched three hours of sleep. I awakened before sunrise to a weird sight in the northeast sky, a comet with its fishtail streaming out from a hazy focus of light. That's a good omen, I thought, and by the time the sun rose like a red basketball *Dove* was on her way under a ballooning main and genoa.

I put my thoughts on the tape recorder:

But there's something missing. There's a great big feeling of emptiness inside this boat. I'm twenty-one but it's hard to fight back the tears. I keep telling myself that this is the last trip and that it'll go much faster than the others.

Anyway, there was a fresh wind on my beam—very unusual in these windless islands—pushing the boat along at five knots. Kili and Fili came on deck together to sniff the weather and the two skinned goats hanging on the shrouds. Piglet and Pooh were still too small to make it up the companionway. On the second day out I cut the goats into parcels (a job I hated) and filled the freezer.

The good wind continued through the second day and I recorded: *Guess someone's looking after me because my spirits are quite buoyant.*

After cleaning the goats' blood off the deck I spent most of the day poring over charts—one for the seas south of Panama and the other for the northern Pacific, which I'd once known well.

On the third day the winds forsook me and the sails began to flop. I stood the calm for a couple of hours and then decided to use power. *Dove* had fuel for three hundred miles and I just wanted to get well away from the Galápagos. If I simply sat around in the doldrums I would go crazy. My plan was to sail close to the equator, due west, for four hundred miles and then due north nine hundred miles past the tiny islands of Clipperton and Clarion. I planned no falls before reaching Long Beach, 2,600 miles away.

It was no use trying to kid myself: this was certainly going to be the toughest leg of the voyage. It was the doldrums I dreaded. I'd heard of some yachts taking more than two months sailing from the Galápagos to California. Two months may not sound like a long time when you're busy. But two months is getting close to forever when you're sailing to the person you love and to the new life that you're hoping for. The sun rises very slowly, and just as slowly the shadows shorten as the heat increases. Then you look at the taffrail-log spinner and it's hanging almost straight down. The afternoon drags by. Then darkness. You sleep. Then you wake up with the sun again and you check your distance. You find you've traveled only thirty miles in twenty-four hours. That's when you think you'll go crazy.

Before disembarking from the *Lina-A*, Patti was scheduled to speak to me by radiotelephone. At the time we'd fixed I tried to get her on the air, but after a frustrating half hour of atmospherics I heard her say, ". . . just can't hear you, honey. But I love you and I miss you. . . . *Lina-A* out."

I did not hear her voice again for nearly a thousand hours, and I couldn't bring myself even to tell the tape recorder how much I missed her. Instead I tried to talk myself into a more positive mood:

Whaddya know, I've gone three hundred miles in five days! That means I'm only two days behind schedule. Okay, I can survive a thirty-four-day sail. Then home! Oh, man! Just think of that! Then what? It has to be something different—something to do with the earth and animals perhaps. Or what about oceanography? I've got a head start here. The main thing I guess is to feed the family. I may have some sort of gift for fixing engines. It might be interesting to study diesels. I always wanted to build houses—not those ugly concrete things, but places where people can really live, houses which smell of timber. A lecture tour? My knees feel like water at the thought of standing up and talking about Fiji or the difference between a halyard and a headstay. It'll work out somehow. It always does. . . . There are so many things I want to learn. . . .

At sea I was a man, but when I thought of the business of making a living in a civilized society I knew I was still a child. I'd seen more races and places than 99.9 percent of my peer group. But I could not picture myself in a world of banks and department stores, of elevators and freeways. I'd never even learned to drive a car!

Of course I knew that life amounted to more than sea horizons, more than how to fix a Hassler wind vane or take an LOP. But I felt I had picked up something which might be useful, something which might even make a contribution to the new thinking, the hopes and goals of young people who are sick of the grab and greed of society.

I'd been long away from the campus but sometimes I felt the vibrations of my peer group. I understood some of the reasons for their revolt. Wasn't my voyage prompted by the same longings for freedom, the same desire to get out of the rut and routine, to prove something to myself—to prove perhaps that a kid doesn't have to be boxed in until he is a mental and spiritual dummy in a business suit?

Unlike a sailboat on a windless ocean, the mind can travel faster than the speed of light—can hover (in my case) like a humming-bird over the thought of "What's for breakfast" and stream away to a comet in the predawn sky and ask, "What or who created that and why and where and when?"

Without another living soul in sight, without so much as a smudge on the horizon, I spent hours and hours simply daydream-ing, just letting ideas and images float across my mind.

"What do you think about at sea?" is one of the questions peo-ple usually ask me. My guess is that I think the same sort of thoughts people think when they walk their dog or take a letter to the mailbox on the corner. The only difference is that at sea you've got more space and time in which to think. You haven't got to return to the office and dig out the pink file on the Jones account or return to the kitchen and peel potatoes. I guess lone sailors should be better philosophers than the guy in apartment 406. Maybe we do get a little closer to the truths, though I cer-tainly did not feel like the wise old man in the mountains.

But I know something about loneliness: Oh, man, I do! I know it can take you close to hell and sometimes, just sometimes, close to heaven.

When people have asked me about being alone and whether they could take it—in the doldrums especially—I've suggested that they should go off by themselves for a couple of days—just two days, say, in a tent out in the sticks. If they like it, if they can keep their own company for forty-eight hours, then they should try being quite alone for a week. That's a real test. If they are able to take that then they might even be able to take forty days in a small boat with only cats for company.

I warn off anyone who hasn't first tried being alone for a few days. Some people will return as raving lunatics.

One "sea thought" I might share here is that life has to have tension—the tension of making another port or finding a piece of gear to mend or how to face a squall. I mean, the guy who is really sick is the guy who has no goal, no ambition, nothing to go for. Having no goal would be like sailing in the doldrums forever.

There are pretty clued-up guys who have thought of these things. I just give this idea as it came to me sitting on the cabin roof in the doldrums under slack sails.

On March 28, after a week at sea, I taped: *Here I am just glaring at these bloody charts and today I can't even raise the energy to eat. I've made sixty miles from noon to noon. Oh, man!*

In the doldrums the very small things became important once again. Playing back the tape recorder you might think I'd struck gold when I reported a big event for Pooh and Piglet. My voice was an octave higher as I shouted: *Whaddya know! The kittens have actually crapped in their own sandbox!*

On Easter Sunday I taped: *Treated myself to a TV turkey dinner. I stuck a couple of candles into bottles and ate the turkey in the cockpit. The wind is so light—actually nonexistent—that the candle flames don't even flicker. Imagine that, here I am in a sailboat and the candle flames on deck look as if they're frozen!*

For my birthday in the Galápagos Patti had given me a model kit of Drake's *Golden Hind*—typical of Patti's care for me. She could have given me a battery shaver or whatever, but she knew that the thing I would need most on the long haul home was something to keep me busy. Gluing the gossamer rigging and the tiny cannons kept me concentrating for many hours. As the model took shape the kittens were determined to destroy it. I would find them chewing off the masts and then I would have to spend more time mending and fixing them up again. That was okay.

I tried to make Patti's saltwater bread and thought I had followed her directions carefully. The loaf felt as if it were made of lead, and I told the tape: *If I eat this stuff I'll have to be careful I don't fall overboard.*

Fresh water was never a problem. Every second or third day there'd be a tropical storm and the rainwater caught in the mainsail ran down the sail track, where I collected it in canvas buckets. There was often enough water to take a sponge bath and to wash out my clothes.

The freezer worked well. It was nice to sit in the tropical sun and to hear ice clinking in my glass. The cats had their own treats when flying fish landed on the deck.

I reported into the recorder: *Fili has fantastic hearing. When there's a plop on deck she's out of the cabin in a flash of fur before the other three cats have stretched their legs.*

The water in the doldrums continued to be glassy smooth, but mentally I dived:

April Fool's day and I'm the fool. This is my ninth day out and I'm only 525 miles from the Galápagos.

I ran into a flat calm yesterday and it's still calm this morning. I started the engine at three forty-five, and ran well in the morning. It's so hot that I'm dripping all the time. I take saltwater showers as often as I can, but when it's hot it's hard to keep clean. I got a breeze in the midafternoon, and for a while I was scooting along at better than six knots. But before midnight it was flat calm again.

It was really awful. I had a sort of breakdown at the end of the day. I had trouble taking down the main. Then I found the boom vang so tightly tied I couldn't undo it. I was working with a flashlight, and I got so mad I went below and threw the flashlight against the bulkhead and broke it. I grabbed a diving knife and went back to cut the jammed line, and I almost slashed the sail up too. Thank heaven I stopped short of doing that because I have no spare sails.

But on April 4 I was awakened by an unusual sound—waves beating against the hull. I leaped through the companionway and hoisted the main and genoa. *Dove* heeled over and I taped: *This is the best day. It's so beautiful. I'm right on course 307 degrees. Wind! Thank God for wind! It has to be the trades!*

That night I saw the North Star for the first time since the Bahamas and next day I caught my first fish since leaving the Galápagos and I also saw my first ship. I recorded in the logbook: "Never thought I'd see a ship out here."

The weather was variable. One day I'd make only thirty miles from noon to noon, but the next I might make as much as eighty.

I had thought that once I'd hit the trades my problems were over. Not so. When the trades died on me I was more depressed than ever. A deep depression is worse than physical pain. Pain is something you can fight, something you can come to grips with. But depression smothers you like a thick fog. You feel it's impossible to fight your way out of it.

After a horrible, endless night I reported into the tape: *Here I am 250 miles from the theoretical doldrum belt and yet there's no wind at all. Last night was absolutely awful. Just horrible dreams. I wouldn't wish a night like last night on my worst enemy. I guess it was a sort of mental breakdown. I just cried like a baby. I've got to beat this thing. It can't go on forever.*

It took three more days before I could even feel the wind again —three days in which I made exactly one hundred miles. The sails flapped and banged—about the ugliest noise a sailor can hear. Apart from nearly driving me crazy, the conditions were hard on the sail seams. But anything was better than just not moving at all, so I kept on trying to sail even when the taffrail-log spinner hung straight down.

Then the sails suddenly filled and I made 149 miles from noon to noon. "Fantastic!" I scrawled across the logbook. I celebrated by cooking a goat's meat roast but some of the meat had turned green. I tried the meat on Fili but she threw up, so I tossed the meat overboard.

On April 12 I saw Clarion island, not much more than a rock, and watched the moon set right behind it. I was worried that a wind change might blow me ashore so I stayed up all night and listened to the radio calls of fishing boats which I guessed were about three hundred miles away. I went to sleep just as the comet appeared in the northeastern sky.

When I awoke at about ten o'clock Fili was missing. This didn't worry me at first, because Fili liked to hide herself away, but after searching in the cabin I knew that Fili was gone. She had traveled half the world with me, this brave, blind cat. I felt sick.

The trades were more constant now and from the southwest. I could choose my course and decided to sail parallel to the coast. Long Beach was still about a thousand miles away. The thermometer suddenly dropped and I could no longer stay on deck and read without being half frozen. The nights were so cold I had to put on long pants and sweaters before getting into bed.

Pooh and Piglet missed their mother and cried but Kili adopted them. When the kittens tried to find out if Kili could give them milk he nudged them over to the food dish. But at night he allowed the kittens to sleep between his paws.

I was pretty sloppy about preparing food, but I ate more on this trip than I'd ever done before. Strangely I did not put on weight. In fact, although I'd grown a couple of inches (to five feet nine) since I'd sailed out of San Pedro in 1965, my weight was exactly the same as when I'd started.

Brewing coffee was quite a ritual. I would measure out the water carefully and let it perk for exactly five minutes. I gave the brew two minutes to cool before pouring my first cup. Then I heated the pot again and took my second cup. I used up quite a lot of fuel on coffee, but it was a luxury I felt I'd earned.

On April 16, my twenty-fourth day at sea, I made radio contact with the fishing boat *Jinita* about two hundred miles away off the Baja California coast. The *Jinita* promised to call up San Diego and get a message if possible to Allen Ratterree, with whom Patti would be staying. I gave them Al's phone number. The thought that I might soon be able to talk to Patti cheered me up a lot. The batteries were a bit low so I went below to start up the engine to charge them. The engine wouldn't start. No engine meant no juice for the radio. Then I saw that I'd forgotten to open up the exhaust pipe.

How dumb can I be? I asked the tape. Guess I'm just too excited. To cool me down I've just made some fudge out of chocolate, sugar and milk all boiled up together. I ought to take out a patent on a new recipe for glue. I tried to make some bread again. This time it has turned out much better but the loaf was as full of holes as a Swiss cheese.

In five years I had succeeded quite well as *Dove*'s captain, navigator and mate, but as Dove's cook I gave myself the sack.

On April 17 I got up early because I wanted to make contact with the *Jinita* again. The fishing boat came through but with the disappointing news that it had failed to make contact with San Diego or Los Angeles. After exchanging weather information, the fishing boat promised to try to contact Los Angeles that night.

Ten minutes later another fishing boat. *Olympia*, came on the air. They'd monitored my call to the *Jinita* and promised to try to raise Al Ratterree. I gave them his phone number.

"Is it important?" asked the *Olympia*.

"Very important," I said.

I kept the radio on, and at seven o'clock that night *Olympia* called back. "We've given your message and position to Mr. Ratterree."

I spoke into the recorder: *Wow, man! That's great! Now at least Patti will know where I am. I feel close to her again.*

Long Beach was only 675 miles away and *Dove* was averaging about one hundred miles a day. But because I was forced to tack, due to headwinds. I was closing the gap by only thirty miles a day. As *Dove* was in the shipping lanes again I had to be careful at night. The masthead light was on the blink—at least it wasn't blinking often enough, because the batteries were low. All through the night I kept a light on deck hoping that the illuminated sails could be seen from a good distance.

I suppose it was because I was getting close to home that I had an unreasoning fear that *Dove* and I were not going to make it. I had read stories of sailors who had been lost on their last voyage. The idea played on my mind that something would happen in the next few hundred miles. It was a real sort of phobia.

My radio reported that three other navigators were making a more dangerous run home than I was. Apollo 13's astronauts, James Lovell, Fred Haise and John Swigert were returning for their Pacific splashdown.

With me it was always a question of keeping up my morale, and on my twenty-fifth day at sea I taped: *Been working on my* model and puttering around with little things. I find a lot to do without doing very much. The weather is gorgeous now—calm and sunny. I got up nerve to take a bath. I really needed it. The water was icy cold, but I got clean. I washed my hair and felt about ten pounds lighter.

At dawn on April 18 I saw land. It was Cape San Lázaro in Baja California. The land was too close for safety so I headed out to sea, hoping for a more favorable wind. Under a reefed main and genoa *Dove* fairly skimmed along. It was just a pity *Dove* wasn't getting any closer to Long Beach, but it was nice to be moving at a good clip.

The weather again changed and became suddenly cold enough to freeze things off a brass monkey. I complained into the tape:

The only time I get really warm is at night. All the three cats come and sleep with me. No wonder! The deck thermometer's in the fifties and all of us are used to the tropics. It's real hard to sleep when itchy little whiskers are tickling your face. . . .

Kili's getting as irritable as I am. There's nothing for him to do —no bugs for him to chase and no green leaves to chew on. The kittens don't seem to mind so much. They are still trying to eat my model ship. They love the threads and the little spools, everything. . . .

Kili seems to be going crazy. He stares at the wall and then his hair goes up as if he's terrified. If I make a quick motion it really wipes him out. I'm wearing a fishing knife in a leather sheath. Kili really hates the leather. Every now and then I feel a little tapping and I look down and there's Kili batting at the sheath. Sometimes he sits down and cries as loud as he can. I don't blame him. There are times when I feel like doing that myself.

For the next five days *Dove* beat into strong headwinds and I made very slow progress. I'd been exactly a month at sea, and Long Beach still looked much too far away. When I had figured I had gone long enough due west I turned toward the coast again.

I taped:

Weather is really terrible now. It's blowing almost a full gale and the sea's much rougher than it's supposed to be. Between noon and noon I made only twenty-five miles toward Long Beach. How stupid can the weather be? Just headwinds. But I can't do much about it. Quite forgot to get my noon latitude sights, but this afternoon took two LOPs which worked out okay. Discovered three chops in the bottom of the freezer. I cooked them in butter and it's the best meal I've had since Patti's stuffed lobster. The cats did well too. I caught a bonita and gave it to them. Can't have the cats looking like alley waifs when we arrive. So we all had quite a party. Been mending a big tear in my Levi's and reading Hailey's Airport.

Next day, April 24, I picked up a more encouraging weather report from San Diego. They forecast that the winds would back from the northwest to the southwest all along the coast. I scrawled in my logbook: Blessed is the Lord. I hope the change comes quickly because I can't take these ceaseless headwinds much longer.

Then a day later my jib halyard broke and I had to jury-rig another, but the wind did swing a bit around the compass and I was able to head northeast, straight for Long Beach. I taped: Slowly getting there, Patti, very slowly, but I'm coming. If the wind holds now, I've got it made.

The wind did hold, and I pushed Dove hard—too hard really for safety. On the night of April 28 I saw a glow in the sky to the north. I knew it couldn't be the sunset. It was the glow from the sprawl of Los Angeles, one hundred miles away. Next morning I passed San Clemente island and picked up the vaguely familiar smell of smog from a city of about ten million people—a raw smell, like wet concrete. For the first time the idea of reaching home really got to me.

I put another reel on my tape recorder: I can't believe it. I don't know what I really feel except that my stomach is all knotted up. Man, I'm tired! It's funny really. This is what I've dreamed about, but I don't know what to say. Just home tomorrow!

I went below and took my first shave since leaving the Galápagos islands. I planned to arrive on the following morning, shortly after dawn, so there was no need to push Dove now.

It was an incredibly beautiful sunset and Dove looked as if she was sailing through a sea of hammered gold. An aircraft came sweeping low several times. It was Bob Madden taking pictures. My radio was tuned to a Los Angeles station and I heard my name on the newscasts.

I used the radiotelephone to call up the Los Angeles Coast Guard, but due to radio "skip" I could only get the Monterey station. I asked them to relay a message to Patti. The Coast Guard said they'd tell Patti that I'd be standing by waiting for her call at ten o'clock that night.

Patti came through on the radiotelephone right on time. It was terrific talking to her again, and yet it was so unreal. She said she had fixed up a temporary room in my parents' home and that she was making the drapes.

I found it hard to think about hanging up drapes. I wondered if I was really dreaming it.

Patti was also finding trouble believing we were close together again. She kept on saying, "Oh, Robin, I can't believe it."

"I can't either," I said.

"It's been so long," said Patti.

"You're not kidding."

"But honestly, Robin, you've made absolutely fantastic speed. We've heard of some boats that have taken ninety days from Galápagos."

"Well, I blew on the sails."

She laughed. It was great to hear her laugh.

Patti said, "The newsmen and the TV people have been chasing us for two weeks. It's really been awful. Try to be nice to them, honey. It won't be long and then we can escape."

"I'll be nice."

"Just keep your cool, please."

"And how's Junior?"

"Oh, he's fine. Swimming around like crazy."

We talked for quite a long time and arranged to meet at the harbor wall an hour after sunrise. *National Geographic* had chartered a big boat and she said she would be on it.

That last night at sea I sat on deck with a quilt wrapped around me to keep out the cold. Occasionally I spoke into the tape recorder: *Okay, boy! I'm now off Pyramid Head.* . . . *Those must be the lights of Santa Catalina, good old romantic Catalina.* . . . *Two o'clock and the moon's just risen. Looks like the moon the cow jumped over.* . . . *Wind is gentle now.* . . . *California, you sure stink! My provisions and supplies have just made it. Same for my endurance.* . . . *Thirty-eight days! Oh, boy!*

Mostly I just thought to myself of the five-year voyage and what it had all added up to.

I'd learned so many things at sea—like kindness has got nothing to do with money and happiness has got nothing to do with rank or race. There were some pretty awful memories, like the time I was nearly run down by a ship at night and the big storm off Malagasy. I thought of the good things too, like the time in the Yasawas and the howl of jackals on the African veld, the thrill of making Mauritius on time under a jury rig and of mending a pelican's beak in the Galápagos.

Little flashes of memory darted through my mind as I sat on deck. I thought how you feel beautiful things deep inside you so that they become part of you.

At sea I had learned how little a person needs, not how much. I wondered why men hold on to life as if the universe depended on them. It seemed to me that so many people hold back from doing the things they really want to do because of fear. The less sophisticated societies seemed to understand this better than the people in the civilized world. Being alone had made me realize that man is pretty insignificant in the universe, like a speck of dust.

I thought how the best times on my voyage were the interludes I had shared with Patti. There were a few periods when I was alone and had enjoyed it. But the loneliness really got to me in the end. Sitting on the deck that last night I admitted to myself that I would not have made the round-the-world voyage if I had not met Patti.

It was a long night and a good time to think. At about three o'clock I went below and took a saucepan bath, changed my clothes and gave the cats an early breakfast. The cats didn't appreciate being waked up so early but they liked the last can of boned chicken.

On April 30, 1970, my thirty-eighth day at sea, I saw the sky lighten in the east. At seven o'clock I sailed past the breakwaters of the port of Los Angeles—1,739 days after I had left them to circle the world alone. I had traveled 30,600 nautical miles.

A powered cruiser came through the mist. Patti was crouched at the forward rail, her blond hair streaming behind her. She was laughing and looking so pretty.

The launch came alongside and Patti leaned over perilously and handed me a breakfast tray set on white linen—half a melon with a cherry in it, cottage cheese, rolls warm from the oven and a bottle of champagne.

Patti couldn't come aboard until I'd cleared customs. Excitement, sleeplessness and champagne made me a bit light-headed. My eyes flooded—and not from the wind. A helicopter hovered overhead (it later crashed but no one was hurt) and then a whole fleet of yachts was heading toward me. It was the start of the annual Ensenada yacht race. As the yachts passed *Dove* the crews shouted and waved welcomes across the water.

At eight o'clock—actually three minutes after—*Dove* nosed into a berth at the Long Beach Marina. I threw a line. *Dove* was tied up. I'd circled the world.

I was glad the customs men kept people off the boat. I sat on the cabin roof while newsmen fired their questions. I wish now that I could have given them better answers, but everything added up to one huge sigh of relief.

Anyway, I didn't really know the answers myself.

"What made you do it?"

There were many reasons. I didn't like school—but that's not unique. I wanted to look at the world, at people and places, without being a tourist. I wanted personal freedom. I wanted to know if I could do something alone—something really difficult. But somewhere deep in my mind I felt there was another reason and that it had something to do with fate and destiny. How could I phrase that? How could I tell these newsmen that I had sailed across the world because I had to do so—because that was what I was meant to do?

Then at last Patti and I were alone. She drove me to our temporary home and hideout. She stopped the car at a traffic light (it was weird seeing traffic lights again) and she said gently, "Robin, it's really just the beginning, isn't it? I mean we have a whole new adventure ahead, a whole new life."

The traffic lights changed from red to green. I was just so tired I couldn't answer her. She understood. She just went on talking quietly.

"It's fantastic to think that we're not going to be apart again . . . and soon there are going to be three of us . . . and all I know is that life is going to be great. . . ."

~~ 12

Child of the Isles

I WOULD BARELY reach the shoulders of John Wayne or Elliot Gould. I can make no rousing speech and I've never rescued anyone from a blazing building or a swollen river. Put twenty people on a stage and ask the audience to pick out the one most likely to walk on Mars or make a billion dollars or find the cure for the common cold and I'd be the last they'd choose. Or perhaps the nineteenth.

So when I saw myself in newspaper blowups under two-inch headlines and staring out of television tubes I felt both fool and fraud. The hardest thing was to fend off newsmen who besieged our small apartment in Newport Beach. National TV channels made attractive offers to tell my story. Appeals came from scores of colleges and schools asking me to lecture.

Then the letters arrived—by the sackload. Many were from foreign countries. We read every one, but we had no secretary and we couldn't answer them all. Some of the letters touched us deeply—like the one from a crippled child who had followed my journey from his hospital cot, and one from a nun who said she'd prayed for me every night. A very moving letter came from a missionary in Taiwan. People of all ages wanted to know how they too could sail around the world, what boat to buy, what ports to call on, how to raise the cash.

Most letters were simple and sincere congratulatory messages from strangers. We were very grateful. There were telegrams and phone calls too.

One phone call came from the Ford Motor Company and invited me to be their "Maverick of the Year." As the gift of a new car went with the title I could hardly refuse. A problem here was that I'd never learned to drive a car and didn't possess a license. Patti promised to remedy this.

There was one contract I had to fulfill. *National Geographic* invited me to Washington to complete the third and last of my three articles for the magazine. They gave me a special reception in Washington and the chairman of the board, Mr. Melville Grosvenor, proposed the toast and handed over a huge colored picture of *Dove*. A chef had turned out a marvelous cake, frosted to show a map of the world and of *Dove* cruising the oceans. It seemed a pity to cut it. I enjoyed reunions with the magazine's photographers and writers who had chased me across the continents, and I thanked them for all the help and the friendship they had given me.

Returning to Long Beach, Patti and I soon began to feel uncomfortable in the city life. We despised the factories which poured stinks and poison into the air, and I soon came across the worst side of human nature. On my voyage I had anchored *Dove* alongside grass-hutted villages and hadn't even bothered to lock the companionway doors. But in Los Angeles harbor thieves broke into *Dove* and stole sails and much valuable equipment. In the Fiji islands I had walked among people whose grandfathers had eaten human flesh, but I first felt afraid of people when I walked at night in the streets of modern cities.

I made another trip across the country, to Detroit this time. The Ford people had arranged a press conference and I showed the newsmen a few slides and answered questions about the voyage. In the evening I was a guest at a dinner where the chief speaker was an astronaut. I was fascinated by his pictures of the moon. Before leaving Detroit they gave me keys to a new Maverick car (actually I didn't pick up the car until I was back in Long Beach).

Patti and I returned to live aboard *Dove* at the marina. We had two big things on our minds—our baby soon to be born and what I was going to do next.

When we had been at Barbados we had received a letter from Doug Davis, one of the deans of Stanford University, who invited me to apply for a special Stanford scholarship. The dean had explained that the university was looking for students "with diverse experiences to balance out the students who had come through conventional academic channels." When I received the letter I wasn't much interested in returning to school. But now Patti and I talked over the idea again. I would know soon enough whether I could take campus life. I phoned the dean and he said at once that the scholarship offer still stood. We would go to Stanford in the fall.

With that question settled, Patti and I joined a special class with other young couples and were taught the skills of prepared (natural) childbirth. The films at first really shook me up, but I soon became fascinated. We were taught the system of rhythmic breathing and how a father could help his wife throughout her labor.

Some parents who had had their babies by what is known as the Lamaze method really impressed us. One of the fathers said: "After the baby was born an incredible calm came over me—it was like I was totally at peace with myself. I drove home slowly from the hospital because I wanted to savor the feeling. I felt extremely lucky to participate in the birth of my son. And my wife and I learned so much about each other too."

We attended six Lamaze classes, and at night in *Dove's* cabin we put in homework on the exercises.

In mid-June Patti's doctor told her that the baby would not

be born before the end of the month, and on June 19 he said it would be okay for us to go sailing and to spend the weekend off Santa Catalina island. We sailed to the island in her father's power boat, the *Jovencita*. The weather was perfect and we stocked up the boat's icebox with the last of our Galápagos lobsters.

After a two-hour trip to the island we moored close to shore. I was surprised when Patti refused to come diving with me. She loved diving. She said she was feeling a bit uncomfortable and decided to stay in the dinghy while I explored the ocean floor. It's terrific diving off Catalina, which is famous for its protected garibaldi fish.

I swam back to the dinghy. Patti was on her hands and knees doing one of the Lamaze breathing exercises. She said, "I've got a rather peculiar backache."

I splashed her with water. "What you need," I replied, "is to loosen up with a swim."

But she wouldn't. "No, honey, I just don't feel like it. I feel just pooped—and if you splash me again I'll clobber you with an oar."

I still didn't suspect anything was wrong. She'd seen the doctor only a few days earlier. He'd been very pleased with her.

It was toward midafternoon. The sun was hot, the water clear as glass. I went on diving and swimming around. Next time I looked over the side of the dinghy I felt the first nag of concern. I'd grown so used to Patti looking like an advertisement for Florida oranges. But now she looked rather strained. She was still doing her breathing exercises in the bottom of the dinghy.

"It's probably nothing," she said a bit too quickly, "but I've just had quite a strong contraction."

"But the doctor told you—"

"Oh, I know he did. But—well—do you think he could be wrong?"

"He'd better not be." I laughed. "I'm all for prepared childbirth, but not in a dinghy."

She smiled. "What about on the rocks—like the iguanas. Remember?"

"Not on the rocks either," I said firmly. "Maybe you should get back to the *Jovencita*."

I paddled the dinghy across to the boat and helped Patti up the ladder. When she was settled on the quarter bunk she said she was fine. I left her for a while, but when I returned I found she was having a contraction.

She didn't smile this time. "Wow, that was quite a strong one!"

Through the porthole the sun was sliding to the horizon.

"Couldn't it be false labor?" I asked.

"Probably," said Patti, "in which case what about some dinner?"

She actually did join Al, Ann and me at the dinner table. The Galápagos lobsters looked terrific. I knew how much Patti enjoyed them, but when she ate only two small mouthfuls I knew there was something really wrong—or really right.

Al volunteered to raise the doctor on the mainland. He got through on the radiotelephone but the doctor wasn't at home. His partner came through eventually.

The partner was very professional, very bedside-manner. He said, "Now if you're worried you can bring your wife to the hospital. But I advise you to wait. First babies usually take their time. It's probably false labor. You just tell her to have a good night's rest."

The doctor didn't seem to understand that we were at least three hours from the hospital, at Huntington Beach—two hours by sea and an hour through the Saturday night traffic.

As I gave Patti the doctor's advice she was again seized with a contraction. It didn't look like false labor to me. But we thought we'd better stick to the medical advice. Al and Ann went to bed.

At two o'clock I realized that unless we acted quickly there was a chance of the baby being born in the cabin of *Jovencita*. At the Lamaze classes they had told us about the things that could go wrong. I didn't tell Patti how worried I was, but I woke up Al. There seemed to be three courses open to us. We could call the Coast Guard helicopter and fly Patti to the hospital, or we could try to sail to the mainland in the *Jovencita*, or again we could see if there was any chance of getting Patti to the tiny little hospital on the island.

We eventually decided to try the Catalina hospital. On the radio Al managed to raise the doctor on duty, who said he would bring an ambulance down to the wharf at Avalon, the harbor on the other side of the island.

Al couldn't get one of the cruiser's engines started, so we limped around the island on one engine while I returned to Patti in the cabin. The time between the contractions was shortening rapidly. Sometimes they were only minutes apart. Patti was really into her breathing exercises. All the things she had needed at the hospital were in the trunk of the car on the mainland. But she did have the stopwatch in her purse. The stopwatch is important equipment in the Lamaze method. The idea is for the husband to time the period between contractions so that he can tell more or less how far along the labor is and what exercises his wife should do. We started the full drill and I massaged Patti's back to relieve the discomfort.

The ambulance and the doctor were at the Avalon wharf. I explained to the doctor how we had been trained in the Lamaze method and that we wanted to be together at the birth.

The doctor nodded. "Yes, yes," he said quickly, "that's all right."

Patti was convinced the doctor was humoring her. She told him hotly, "I'd rather have the baby on the boat than go to the hospital and you not allow Robin to stay with me."

She made the doctor promise I could stay with her right through her labor before she would get into the ambulance. She made him promise that he wouldn't give her any drugs.

We were luckier with the doctor than we had dared to hope. He was quite young and had just returned from a spell of practicing medicine in Alaska. He had seen Eskimos have babies and he was enthusiastic about natural childbirth.

We looked pretty primitive as we shuffled barefooted into the eight-room hospital. We had no spare clothes—just a couple of toothbrushes. There was a nice nurse on duty who gave us a real welcome. Births are rare on Catalina. The nurse gave me paper overshoes two sizes too big and a white coat for the delivery room. Patti put on a linen thing with tabs at the back. The adventure of childbirth was suddenly exciting again.

Patti's contractions were now separated by seconds. The nurse was puzzled because in the book she should have been moaning and crying out. Patti never whimpered. She was totally absorbed in what she was doing. I was amazed at her courage. She didn't talk much. She sometimes held my hands very tightly. The doctor didn't even unseal his hypodermic syringe.

Quimby's birth was the most terrific experience of our lives. Actually it was quite a long labor, but whenever Patti forgot her different breathing exercises I was there to remind her what to do —slow and easy between contractions, medium breathing as the contractions moved to a climax.

I am no expert on childbirth and I know things can go wrong. But I know that Quimby's birth is how a birth is meant to be.

Somewhere along the trail of man's evolution to the electronic age the secret has been lost. For millions childbirth has become a horror of pain and fear and drugs. Most mothers in "civilized" societies are hardly aware of what should be the most fulfilling moment of their lives. Most fathers are hidden away in tobacco-filled rooms with worn carpets. Most parents go through hell until a stranger reeking of anesthetics tells them they have a son or daughter.

It wasn't that way for us. I was there to tell Patti the moment Quimby's head appeared. I was there to announce that our baby had ten fingers. Then, after a surge like the highest wave of a full tide upon a beach, I told Patti, "It's a Quimby!" This was a name we had once mentioned in the Galápagos.

When Quimby came out of the darkness and saw the light of her first earth day she did not need to be slapped to force her to take a gulp of air. On her own she did it, because she was as drug free as her mother. Quimby was separated from Patti and I picked her up, pink, slippery, unbruised by forceps, crying with life.

There were three of us now, three of us bound together by love and the richest of all human experiences.

Patti's face was wan and drawn, but she managed a marvelous smile as she reached out and touched her daughter's hand. Then she reached up her arms to me and I buried my face in her hair. Both of us wept, not with pain.

"Thank you, honey," she whispered.

"And you," I said.

"I couldn't have done it without you," she said.

"I had the easy part."

I left her then to rest and went out into the early morning sun, glistening off white cottages and the sea beyond. In front of one cottage there was a garden full of flowers, and near the wall a rose, pink and perfect, the dew still on the petals.

On sudden impulse I pushed open the garden gate, walked the short drive and knocked on the door. A woman, gray-haired and in a robe, appeared. She looked startled.

"There's a rose in your garden, the one near the wall. May I have it? I'll buy it," I said.

The woman pursed her lips. "Oh, I don't sell roses, and the one you're pointing at is the best in my garden."

"I need it for my wife," I said, and then I told her of the events of the night and of the birth of Quimby.

She listened in silence, then disappeared into the house and returned with some scissors.

"I've got some more roses at the back," she said. "Your wife deserves more than one."

"No," I said, "just one—just that one."

The woman walked across her garden and snipped off the perfect rose. I returned to the hospital with the single bloom. They'd moved Patti into a small room filled with sunlight, and with a view of mountains and very green grass—not another building in sight. Patti was lying quietly. The color had returned to her cheeks. She looked as if she'd been lying in the sun all day. She was not asleep. The nurse found a thin-stemmed vase and I put the rose on the table beside Patti's bed. She didn't say anything but her eyes followed me around the room and then settled on the rose.

That evening the doctor told us it was rare to see such an easy delivery in modern society. He questioned us closely on the techniques we had learned together.

The hospital people waived the rules and allowed me to stay in the room with Patti for the next two days. Then on Monday morning the three of us, Patti and I and the child of the isles, flew back to the mainland in a small seaplane.

~~~ 13

Home from the Hill

IN THE FALL we put a "For Sale" sign on *Dove* and drove up to Stanford University, just south of San Francisco. It must be one of the most beautiful campuses in the world. We had grown so used to tropical vegetation that we'd forgotten what autumn colors looked like. We'd forgotten the smell of woodsmoke.

Our car was no longer looking Detroit-new because when I was learning to drive I had tried to apply the techniques of a rudder to the steering column and had had an argument with a gravel truck. We soon sold the patched-up car and invested in a retired mail van with about 100,000 miles on the clock. The old blue van better suited our personalities, and besides it could easily be converted into a camper in case we decided to escape.

On an estate not far from the campus we found a small cabin tucked away behind tall trees. The cabin had one room, with a big red brick hearth. We salvaged an iron bed from a junkyard across the tracks, put some of our Yasawa shells on the windowsill and settled Quimby on the floor with her favorite toy—the car keys.

Until *Dove* was sold we would have to live off my earnings from odd jobs around the campus. When I came home on the second day with a basketful of fruit and vegetables I did not at first tell Patti that I had found them in the trash bins behind the local supermarket. For the next four months we did not pay a cent for fruit and vegetables. The supermarket throw-outs were almost good enough for the White House—except for the beans. For some reason the beans were always stringy.

I vaguely planned on an engineering degree with architecture as the goal. There were several reasons why we saw through only one semester at Stanford. I should have guessed that having quit school at the age of sixteen I would have trouble returning to school at twenty-one. Actually I did take my work seriously, even though I'd forgotten how to spell *algebra*.

What surprised us most was how little we had in common with our peer group because most of them had grown up in a different world. I had had the advantage of experiences that most people don't gain in a lifetime and I'd seen horizons far beyond the local ball park and movie theater. It was sad to see how some students straight from high school were ready to believe anything and were so easily duped by cynical professors, especially by one Maoist who was passionate about his bloody revolution. The students who applauded this professor loudest were the ones who owned the Porsches and the Jags.

We made some good friends among the faculty and the students. Most of the students genuinely wanted to see society changed for the better. Like Patti and me, they wanted to expose hypocrisy and they despised the brainwashing attempts to persuade my generation that the dollar buys the only important things in life.

It certainly wasn't Stanford's fault that Patti and I couldn't fit into the campus life. It's a great school and we knew how lucky we were to be there. But right from the start we had a feeling of claustrophobia. The walls of the classroom boxed me in so that I could hardly breathe. I began to fear that even if I saw through my years at the university I would be sucked into a life style which

Patti and I were determined to avoid—the nine-to-five routine, membership in the country club and that sort of thing. That first semester at Stanford seemed as long as two years at sea.

After an especially frustrating day in which, among other things, I had had to listen to the Maoist professor talk about his new society ("Everyone will be equal and thieves will be treated in a hospital"), I returned to our cabin convinced that we were on the wrong track. We went to bed that night by firelight and talked into the small hours. At about three in the morning we decided it was time for us to move on.

We would go to some place where we could find the simple life we had so often dreamed of and talked about; some place where we could tame the land as our forebears had done and really prove our self-sufficiency.

"We'll teach Quimby to love trees and grass and animals and mountains," said Patti. "That's the way we planned it, remember."

"And we won't have to listen to the kind of crap I heard today," I said.

Patti's head was on my shoulder. She said, "You mean where the bull is for real."

I felt her laughing softly. The firelight darted tongues of amber across the cabin ceiling.

A couple of days later we packed everything into the postal van and chugged back to Los Angeles to finalize the sale of *Dove*. This and other business took longer than we expected and once again fate seemed to play the cards. Or was it fate?

We had no fixed idea of where to go—just somewhere where the air was clean, where there were mountains, water, trees and, most importantly, where people didn't live on top of each other. We looked at the map of Canada and made inquiries about home-steading, but we didn't really want to lose our American citizenship. For better or for worse this was our country and so we circled the states where the towns were widely spaced and the roads were thin. Montana fitted our picture.

The most important thing that happened to us during our brief return to Los Angeles is really hard to put into words. One Sunday evening my cousin David took us to a new kind of church attended by five thousand people of all ages. It was the first time we had been to any sort of religious meeting in as long as we could remember. Patti and I were on guard.

We didn't have any sudden conversion or anything like that, but we were fascinated by the sincerity and the obvious happiness of the people alongside us and by those who spoke. We sensed something exciting was happening, something which we hadn't even guessed at. It was like seeing the beginning of a renaissance in which the real values were being recognized again.

This meeting was so different from my fixed ideas about church. It was a non-denominational service and the people around us seemed to be of every race and background. The people who spoke talked about God and Jesus as if they were real and contemporary and living, and not just stained glass images. We didn't at first want to believe anything because we feared that religion would complicate our lives. But the young people, especially, seemed to have a faith and a hope and a love that we envied.

That night when we went to bed we took out the Bible I had bought in New Guinea, the one I had covered with a detective story jacket. We read aloud to each other. The Bible began to make sense. In fact it really turned us on. There were ideas here which filled an empty place in our thinking.

When we had stopped reading we began to talk about the things that had happened to us in the previous five years. We had put these all down to fate—like the times I'd come pretty close to death and my meeting up with Patti in the Fijis.

Patti asked, "Do you think fate is really God?"

"I don't know," I said. "Someone was sure looking after me."

"I think someone helped us to meet as we did," said Patti.

We remembered the letter we had received from the missionary in Taiwan, and Patti took it out of the box of correspondence we'd filed away. We reread the letter and we were especially interested in the last paragraph. The missionary had said, "Your story will help others to find the right way for their lives."

Our finding a belief in God—becoming Christians—was a slow thing. We felt our way forward very carefully. Before that evening, if anyone had mentioned God or Jesus we would have walked the other way and been careful to avoid that person in the future. But now we wanted to meet people who would help us understand more about what we read in the Bible. We wanted to learn how to work out our lives in the way God intended us to. In reading the Bible together we were fascinated by the prophecies made two thousand years and more ago, prophecies which seemed to be coming true, like the Jews returning to their own country.

We have no idea where these new thoughts and ideas and practices will take us and no desire at this point to join a structured church society. But we are open to whatever direction God will give us. Our belief is simple. It is the belief that so many of our own generation are discovering—a belief that God isn't dead as some of the older generation have told us. In a world that seems to be going crazy we are learning that Jesus showed men the only way they should live—the way we were meant to live.

When the sale of *Dove* was fixed up, we packed all our possessions into the mail van and headed north. We felt sure now that we would know where to go. It was a spring morning and our last view of Los Angeles was of a huge factory pouring so much stink and poison into the air that it blotted out the sun. That evening we traveled through the desert country and it looked marvelous. When darkness came some small wild animals were caught in our headlights. We took turns driving and when we hit the snow we had some trouble. But people came and helped us, and one old man knelt in the snow and helped me change a wheel. Even the people were different.

Two days later the mail van carried us into Montana. The hills and the mountains rose up ahead and the trees came down to meet us. We knew we were near the land we were seeking. We traveled slowly, just looking about, getting the feel of the mountains and lakes and smelling the pine-scented air. It was fantastic! In the next week we spent a lot of time with realtors—the good ones and the bad ones. With Quimby in my arms, we tramped over hundreds of acres and then, halfway up a mountain, we found a spot overlooking a lake.

There wasn't another building in sight. It seemed like the most beautiful place we had ever seen. Sunlight poured through the trees and the first spring flowers were pushing up the earth. We knew this was the place where we would build our home.

The money from the sale of *Dove* allowed us to buy 160 acres. Our nearest neighbors were three miles away. We followed the fresh spoor of deer, elk and moose into the forest.

We didn't kid ourselves that there wasn't plenty of hard work ahead. I started at once to build a temporary lean-to cabin from timber left at a disbanded lumber mill. We began to clear an area of forest to allow us to plant vegetables and flowers and fruit trees.

In the next six weeks we stayed in the village while I took a course in logging, learning the different trees, how to fell them and measure their board feet. In winter we would be snowed in and it would be a time to test our skills, our faith and our courage in creating a new and simple life style. With the help of a correspondence course we plan to educate Quimby ourselves. She will go at her own pace and she will learn to love the earth and to protect it.

We don't think of ourselves as running away from civilization but as apprentices learning to enjoy the natural world. We believe that God will help us to understand how we are meant to live.

We have made friends with our neighbors, even though they live so far away. In this country people need each other. One day we returned to the lean-to and found a hamper of food at the door. One of the neighbors had called and left us homemade cheese, homebrewed wine and other things. After exploring the gifts, Patti looked at me and said, "And now, Robin, when are you going to provide the meat?"

The idea sent her into a gale of laughter. Holding Quimby by the hand, she said, "I'm thinking what would make great last lines to the first part of our life story."

"Yes?"

"Well," said Patti, "I can see you coming down that trail with an elk over your shoulder, and Quimby and I will be standing just like this in front of our new log cabin."

"Go on," I said.

"And then I'll quote those words you found on the grave of Robert Louis Stevenson in Samoa. Remember them?"

"Sure," I said, laughing too.

> Home is the sailor, home from the sea,
> And the hunter home from the hill.